The Healthy Firehouse Cookbook

The Healthy Firehouse Cookbook

Low-Fat Recipes from America's Firefighters

Joseph T. Bonanno, Jr.

Hearst Books / New York

This book is dedicated to six special people, five of whom I lost to fire: my mother, Audrey Bonanno, who died from critical burns sustained at home; my dear friend Firefighter Richard Karnik; Firefighter Barry Feeney, Firefighter Sal Fenech, and Lieutenant James Tonry, who died from job-related cancers; and Firefighter Anthony Parella. This book is also dedicated to all firefighters everywhere, especially those who have given the supreme sacrifice.

Library of Congress Cataloging-in-Publication Data

Bonanno, Joseph T., Jr.
    The healthy firehouse cookbook : low-fat recipes from America's firefighters / Joseph T. Bonanno, Jr.
      p. cm.
    Includes index.
    ISBN 0-688-12755-X
    1. Low-fat diet—Recipes. I. Title.
RM237.7.B66 1995
641.5'635—dc20   94-28182
                                           CIP

Printed in the United States of America

2   3   4   5   6   7   8   9   10

BOOK DESIGN BY RICHARD ORIOLO

Acknowledgments

I would like to thank Gary Goldberg of the New School, without whom this book might never have happened. His excellent course "How to Write a Cookbook and Get It Published" was the beginning of this book. Harriet Bell for acknowledging my idea in class and turning it into a reality. Susan Ginsberg, my agent, for being part agent, part tutor, part psychologist through the whole publishing process. Rick Rodgers for all his help in turning firehouse recipes of "a little bit of this and a whole lot of that" into cookbook format and for all his tips on cooking and recipe writing. Delores Custer for her help in recipe writing. Mary Johnson of *McCall's* magazine for her tremendous job of nutritional analysis of the recipes. Marialisa Calta for her excellent article in *Eating Well* magazine, "Healthy Heroics," on a night in the firehouse, meal included. Mary Goodbody for her help in turning firehouse slang into literature. My neighbors Eddie and Joann Burke and sons Ed and Brian for tasting and testing my at-home recipes. Cynthia and Helen Levas for all their help in preparing the proposal for this book.

A special thanks to all the members of Engine 273 and Ladder 129 in Flushing, Queens, for putting up with my recipe testing on them. I thank them all from the bottom of my heart for their input as food critics. Though a bit blunt, they were above all honest in their opinions and not shy about letting me know how a meal tasted.

More special thanks to all the firefighters who donated recipes for this book and to all the people who helped me along the way.

Contents

A Fireman's Poem

I have no ambition in the world, but one
and that is to be a fireman.
The position, in the eyes of some,
may appear to be, a lowly one
but we, who know the work a fireman has to do,
believe his is a noble calling.
Our proudest moment is to save . . . Lives.
Under the impulse of such thoughts
the nobility of the occupation thrills us
and stimulates us to deeds of daring,
even of supreme sacrifice.

—Edward F. Crocker
Chief of Department
NYFD
1899–1911

Introduction

Although I made the decision to become a firefighter more than fifteen years ago, I remember it as if it were yesterday. I based that decision on one undeniable fact: young or old, every firefighter I had ever met was happy. I have since learned that the happiness comes from loving life to the fullest because we are constantly reminded that we may not be around in the morning to enjoy the simple things everyone takes for granted.

My father was a firefighter, but he never pressured me to become one. On the contrary, I was encouraged to weigh the pros and cons of various career choices. Nevertheless, I still remember the field trip my elementary school class took to the local firehouse, where I stared wide-eyed at the fire trucks and firefighters, almost frightened by the size of both and practically hypnotized by the sounds and smells of the firehouse. After such a trip every boy wants to grow up to be a firefighter, and quite honestly, I didn't really believe that some twenty years later I would be wearing the boots, coat, and helmet of a New York City firefighter.

I grew up in the South Bronx, which at that time was a nice place to live. I remember the smell of burned-out buildings and smoke on my dad's clothing, but my brothers and I never felt firefighting was our destiny. The only exposure we had to the people he worked with was at social events such as firehouse picnics in the park, where we ate good food, played games, and had lots of fun. I grew up thinking of firefighters as great, happy-go-lucky guys.

After college, while considering other careers and urged on by friends, I took the test to qualify as a New York City firefighter. Thirty-eight thousand applicants took the same test, and I was one of the 7,500 who passed. I scored well on the written exam, got into top physical condition, and scored high on the physical exam too. I was selected from a candidate list as one of 4,000 of the original 7,500 who, over the next four years, were eventually hired.

I spent eight weeks at a military-style boot camp, after which I was assigned to a firehouse as a probationary firefighter, or "probie." At boot camp we learned how to maintain and operate the equipment, how to enter a burning building, and how to react in a fire to the countless situations we might encounter. I remember having to crawl on my belly through a seemingly endless smoke-filled building and finally emerging into fresh air, only to be ordered back inside by an unsmiling instructor. Coughing and sputtering, face blackened and throat burning, I did it again. This was not cruel or unreasonable. This training was necessary preparation for battling actual fires.

Once I was assigned to a firehouse, my education continued under the watchful eyes of veteran firefighters. I learned the day and evening routines for checking equipment, taking turns at the alarm desk, and other firehouse duties. I adjusted to sleeping at the firehouse when necessary, and, yes, I mastered sliding down a fire pole! I also learned that the break from the routine in any firehouse is the meal. This is a special time when we sit down as a big family to eat, laugh, and savor some firehouse cuisine. Firefighting, with its close association with death and destruction, gives firefighters an unparalleled love of life, so that they enjoy everything to the fullest, especially food.

I ate many wonderful meals cooked by veteran firefighters; however, as the months went on, it became apparent that they paid no attention whatsoever to the amount of fat they used or the nutritional content of their meals. Butter was added in mass quantities to everything. Because I was a probie, my initial suggestions for more healthful food brought remarks such as "You can't put out fires on a stomach full of bean sprouts," "I'm a meat-and-potatoes kind of guy," and "I want something that will stick to my ribs." The trouble was, their high-fat meals were sticking to the inside of their arteries, not their ribs. I accepted that I could die in a fire, but I didn't want to die from injuries sustained at the kitchen table.

This was the beginning of my crusade to improve the diets of my friends and colleagues—and myself. These experienced firefighters taught me how to stay alive in a fire; I wanted to show them how to stay alive by exercising regularly and eating well. I began to exclude myself from typical firehouse meals and started cooking my own low-fat meals, enduring skepticism and numerous "witty" remarks about doing so. But when two of the firefighters in my firehouse required bypass surgery, suddenly even the most cynical veteran became interested in my cooking.

One by one, I gradually convinced the veterans that a nutritious meal can be delicious, low in fat and cholesterol, and perhaps most important, of substantial proportion to satisfy the legendary hearty appetites of firefighters. The veteran cooks began to bring a healthy recipe or two from home, began to experiment with reducing the fat in some classic dishes, and paid more attention to fruits and vegetables. Many of them began to exercise regularly and found they could lose the pounds it had taken years to accumulate without starving. They discovered that diets don't work and that fitness and health are just matters of exercising regularly and learning how to prepare heart-healthy meals.

Because I was enjoying this interest in healthy eating, I was inspired to take a cooking course in low-fat cooking. As I was investigating the various courses available in New York City (and there were lots!), I noticed a one-day seminar on cookbook writing offered at the New School. I was free that day and so, on a whim, I went.

I was one of about sixty people, and it seemed as if everyone else knew what he or she was doing. There were questions about agents, contracts, and publishing rights. People had proposals drafted and manuscripts in hand. I sat there fascinated, thinking that I would make a beeline for the door when it was over. I was out of my league.

Early in the day we had gone around the room, each person stating briefly his or her idea for a book. I said something about a firefighter healthy-eating book, mentioning that I was, in fact, a New York firefighter. To my astonishment, at the end of the workshop one of the panelists, a man named Gary Goldberg, asked me more about it. Next, I found myself talking to Harriet Bell, my editor, who seemed genuinely interested and suggested I find an agent and write a proposal.

Once I had a contract, I advertised in *Firehouse Magazine*, asking my fellow firefighters to share healthy recipes. I also compiled my own and those of my friends. These are the recipes you will find on the following pages.

Firefighting is a tough job done by tough people. The rigors of the job demand a hearty meal, but hearty does not have to mean unhealthy. More than 500,000 Americans die each year from coronary heart disease, directly related in many cases to diet. The firehouse recipes in this book are nutritious and easy to prepare, and will stick to your ribs—not your arteries. Nearly every one derives less than 30 percent of its calories from fat and has been tested in a firehouse kitchen. This means it satisfies the most demanding food critics of all: hungry firefighters!

A Brief History of Firehouse Cooking

As early as 1923 a Massachusetts fire chief was quoted in *Firehouse Magazine* praising firehouse cooking: "The experiments which have taken the form of new fangled ideas in cookery have met with such apparent success that there has been little or no sickness among the firemen this year; . . . such progress should be encouraged." A few years earlier the same magazine had sent two women to eat in a firehouse, who reported that the meal was impressive and the dining room "rare and spotless."

Clearly, by the 1920s firehouse cooking was a firmly established practice that continues to this day. Firefighters began cooking for each other early in the 1800s, when only volunteer departments existed in large cities. In those days, when the railroads were new, firefighters traveled between cities to visit other volunteer departments and compare notes on operation. Whenever out-of-towners arrived, they were feted with a banquet.

During the Civil War the New York firefighters formed the first volunteer military outfit, the First Fire Zouaves. Eleven hundred strong, the Zouaves saw action at Bull Run and other battlefields. In 1861, while stationed in Washington, D.C., they assisted in putting out a fire next to the famous Willard Hotel and were honored at a banquet by the grateful hotel management. Unhappily, the Zouaves were better equipped to fight fires than to battle Confederate soldiers and returned to New York with fewer than three hundred men.

By the end of the Civil War, New York City established the nation's first paid fire department, called the New York–Brooklyn Metropolitan Fire Department. Hiring preference was given to the volunteers, and by 1865 the department had six hundred paid firemen, thirty-three engines, and eleven ladder apparatuses and was divided into companies of twelve men. The men worked constantly, with three one-hour meal breaks per day and one day off per month, for an annual salary of $700.

During these early days the firehouse was used mainly to house the horses and equipment. By 1920 motorized fire apparatus replaced horses and the firehouses were remodeled. Haylofts became sleeping quarters, and former horse stalls were dismantled to make way for kitchens and dining areas. The companies adopted the platoon system, in which the men alternated day and evening shifts and had to eat at least one meal at the firehouse. One man was appointed to cook and others to assist. It did not take long for firehouse food to gain a reputation as being hearty, plentiful, and delicious.

Today every firehouse in the country has a kitchen, most of which are used to prepare meals. Certainly, firefighters around the nation resort to take-out meals from time to time, but more often than might be expected, they cook from scratch, taking great pride in their food.

In my company in Flushing, Queens, we shop and cook together. It is not unusual to see several firefighters roaming the aisles of the local supermarket, comparing prices on meat, chicken, and fresh produce. We even communicate with each other on our radios, checking on prices or the location of certain items! We pool money to buy the groceries for the meal, and donate a small amount each month to keep the kitchen stocked with staples such as salt, pepper, cooking oil, ketchup, paper towels, dishwashing detergent, and the like.

Firefighting is a job that requires constant vigilance. We cannot leave the firehouse for very long or be out of reach by radio. At any time an alarm can come in that requires fast action and speed. Even so, there is a lot of down time that is often spent working out in the firehouse basement, studying, checking equipment, or perhaps best of all, planning and cooking meals.

Fire Safety in the Kitchen

The fact that approximately twelve thousand Americans (at least one hundred of whom are firefighters) die every year in fires should make all of us aware of the real dangers of fires. This number exceeds the number of people killed by natural disasters, including floods, hurricanes, and earthquakes. We in the United States have the highest per-capita fire death rate in the industrialized world. In addition, fifty thousand people are hospitalized every year because of fire-related injuries and burns and remain hospitalized on average from four weeks to two years.

At greatest risk for death from fire are children and the elderly. Fire deaths and injury are twice as high for men as for women. Fire kills more children than all forms of childhood cancer and is second only to automobile accidents as the leading cause of death for children under age five; for children between the ages of five and fourteen, it ranks third, following car accidents and drowning, as causes for death.

Preventing Fires in the Kitchen and the Rest of the House

Cigarettes are the leading cause of residential fires and consequently of residential fire deaths. This fact often is not included in statistics about deaths caused by smoking. More fires begin in the kitchen than anywhere else in the house. Cooking accidents cause most apartment fires and, after cigarettes, most single-family home fires. Cooking accidents account for about 130,000 fires every year in residences, and it's estimated that approximately 16 percent of the fatal fires in the United States begin in the kitchen.

Because the kitchen is a potentially dangerous area, it is only sensible to take precautions. Most kitchen fires start because of carelessness and unattended stoves rather than faulty equipment.

Smoke Detectors A working smoke detector doubles your chances of surviving a fire, and all houses and apartments should be equipped with several. In residential fires, nine out of ten of the children who die live in homes without smoke detectors. At any given time it is estimated that half the homes with smoke detectors have ones that are not functional. They have either a bad electrical connection, dead batteries, or no batteries at all. Probably the best kind of smoke detector is an electric one with a battery backup. Check the batteries regularly, about every six months. For some people, it's easy to remember to do this at the same time you change the clocks twice a year for daylight saving time.

Smoke detectors should be on all floors and in strategic places, such as near stairwells. Do not put one so close to the stove that it goes off with little provocation. You will probably pull the battery from it and never replace it. It's important to have a smoke alarm at ceiling height in the kitchen, however. Consider buying one with a reset button so that you can turn it off when you're cooking something that sets it shrilling. It still may go off when you occasionally burn something, and while the piercing noise is obnoxious, imagine how comforting it will seem if it is the sound that enables you to get your children out of the house in the middle of the night.

Fire Extinguishers Fire extinguishers are special pressurized devices that release chemicals or water to aid in putting out fires. They keep small fires from spreading until the fire department can arrive and may help provide an escape route for you and your family. Install a working Class ABC extinguisher in the kitchen, mounted on a bracket where you can easily reach it (not in a drawer or the back of a cupboard). These extinguishers contain dry chemicals and will handle fires caused by wood and paper (Class A), fires caused by grease or flammable liquids (Class B), and electrical fires (Class C). You can get UL-rated ABC New Halon extinguishers, which use a liquefied gas called halon, for maximum effectiveness and no residual mess. They are more expensive than other extinguishers, however.

A five-pound extinguisher should be ample for kitchen fires and is easy to handle; larger extinguishers can handle more fire, but if you cannot handle them, they are next to useless. Make sure the extinguisher you buy has a pressure gauge and check it about once a month. Learn how to use the extinguisher—reading the instructions once the fire has started won't do you much good. Finally, don't mount the extinguisher near the stove. If the flames are leaping from a pan or the oven, you may not be able to reach over them to get to the extinguisher.

Stoves When it comes to stoves, most cooks have a cooking preference, and many seem to prefer gas to electric. Those with no choice or no preference adapt to whatever type is in the apartment or house when they move in. Although both stoves cook food satisfactorily, electric stoves are slightly safer than gas simply because there is no exposed flame or combustible gas.

Despite this, electric stoves pose their own hazards. The coils are silent and, unless on full heat, do not look "hot." This means it's not terribly unlikely that someone could touch one that is still hot enough to burn. If a pan is too small for the coil and leaves part of it exposed, it's possible for a dish towel, grabbed in haste instead of a pot holder, to catch on fire. The exposed coil can also heat a pan handle so that it burns your hand. Especially lethal are the newer electric stovetops that are completely smooth. They are easy to keep clean but have few or no visible signs to warn you that they are turned on and hot. There are cases of babies, left for just seconds on a kitchen counter, during a diaper change, for instance, who have crawled over these smooth surfaces and suffered second- and third-degree burns. With any electric stove, be sure all burners are turned completely off when you finish cooking.

Electric ovens with the heating elements on top are dangerous too, particularly if they are situated under the stove so that the elements are at an angle where they might come into contact with forearms and wrists, the edge of a dish towel, or an oven mitt.

Gas stoves, wonderful for adjusting the heat during cooking, can cause problems because of the open flame. Do not use loose towels to retrieve pots and pans and be aware of loose hair, shirttails, and flowing sleeves that might brush the flame. If your stove is of the vintage to have a pilot light, make sure it is always on. Do not use the stove top as a countertop. The pilot light has enough heat to ignite grocery bags temporarily left on the stove top. Learn how to light it safely in case it goes out. When igniting a gas burner, never leave the gas on for more than a few seconds while waiting for it to light—and never attempt to light it with a match. Few things invite accidents more than fumbling with matches around a gas stove. Lighting a gas oven with a match is an even greater invitation for disaster: the gas fumes are contained in a smaller area, which increases opportunity for an explosion. Also, do not use the kitchen for crafts that involve flammable glues or thinners. In a confined area the pilot light can ignite their fumes.

Gas stoves also are dangerous because of the explosive fuel needed to run them. Make sure that bottled gas lines are secure and unobstructed and that the tanks or bottles are on secure platforms and chained to prevent them from toppling over.

If the pilot light goes out and you smell gas, or if you smell gas when you open the oven door or walk into the kitchen, immediately call the fire department. Shut off the gas supply if you can, open the windows, and get out of the house.

It's important to have two shut-off valves for the gas lines to the cooktop and oven. On the stove itself, a good place is under the lift-off lid; the other shut-off valve should be out of the kitchen but easily accessible to you and a firefighter—perhaps within easy reach in the basement or attached garage. This is important in case a fire makes the kitchen inaccessible. If there is not another shut-off, the firefighters may have to wait for the gas company to arrive to turn off the gas outside the house, losing valuable time that could be used to extinguish the fire.

Dealing with Kitchen Fires

One of the most common causes for small kitchen fires is igniting grease or oil. Hot oil and grease can light up instantly, particularly if permitted to heat to their smoking points. Keep pot lids nearby when cooking with oils; if the contents of a pan catch on fire, smother the flames with the lid. You might also invest in a small asbestos fire blanket, available in most hardware stores, to keep near the stove for smothering flames.

Never attempt to carry a flaming pan outdoors or to the sink. You may spill the contents and spread the fire. Or you may spill it on yourself and cause serious burns. Leave it where it is, turn off the burner, and smother the flame with the lid, fire blanket, or fire extinguisher. Never pour water on a grease fire.

If grease in the broiler or oven catches fire, turn off the heat and smother the flame with a fire blanket or use an extinguisher. Sometimes closing the door to the oven cuts off enough oxygen to kill the flames.

Neither baking soda nor salt is particularly effective in putting out grease fires. Fire extinguishers and smothering devices (pot lids, fire blankets) work better and generally are easier to reach and use.

Keep stoves and ovens, whether they are gas or electric, clean and grease-free. Caked-on grease can ignite with little warning, and it may be in the back of the broiler, on the oven floor, or in the heating elements, where you do not see it every day. Check under the burners for dripped grease. It's equally important to keep your pots and pans clean. Setting a greasy-bottomed pan on a burner is dangerous.

Never cook and drink alcohol at the same time. The majority of our calls for kitchen fires come from homes where the cook has been drinking. This may happen because the inebriated cook falls asleep before the food is cooked or simply because intoxication makes him or her far less careful than usual.

As a final word of caution, I strongly recommend that every kitchen be equipped with a telephone. Numerous kitchen fires begin when pots are left unattended, frequently because the cook leaves the kitchen to answer the phone, becomes involved in the conversation, and only remembers there is something on the stove when the smoke from a fire reaches the other room. If you must talk on the phone while cooking, do so in the kitchen.

Preventing Burns

If you examine a chef's hands, you will most likely see countless small scars and red patches, the remnants of burns. Small burns may be an occupational hazard of making your living in a kitchen, but even the most cavalier chef knows how to take precautions to avoid serious burns. Home cooks should too.

Use thick oven mitts for lifting pans from the oven and pots off the stove. Pot holders are better than nothing, but because they leave a good portion of your hand and wrist exposed, they are less satisfactory. Neither mitts nor pot holders are fireproof, and so you must take care not to leave them near the stove. Use oven mitts and pot holders when taking dishes from the microwave. The appliance does not generate "heat," but it does cause the food to cook and get hot, which in turn heats up the dish in which it cooks.

Know how heavy a pot is. Do not attempt to lift a full pan from the stove with one oven-mitted hand if you might need two hands. The natural reaction to a heavy pot is to grab it with your other hand. If the pot is hot, there is potential for three accidents: first, you may burn the unprotected hand; second, you may drop the hot pan and burn another part of your body; and third, if there is oil or grease in the pan, it may ignite and cause a fire.

Do not use dish towels to lift pans from the stove or oven. Trailing cloth can easily ignite. The same goes double for paper towels or napkins. Don't use gardening or work gloves in place of oven mitts. They are not as thick, and if they catch fire, they are harder to remove because they have fingers. An oven rack stick fitted with notches is a handy tool for pulling and pushing oven racks out of and into the oven.

Set pans on the stove with their handles turned away from another ignited burner. This keeps them cool and prevents accidental burning. Use the right size pan for the job. Overfilled pans may bubble over and, depending on the contents, cause fires. This advice applies to pans for cooking in the oven too. If there is danger of a boil-over in the oven, set a larger pan beneath the smaller one to catch the hot liquid. Take care when removing lids from pans full of boiling liquid—hot steam causes burns.

Hot water can burn too. Keep the hot-water heater turned to no higher than 120°F. At 145°F, a mere 25° hotter, water can scald skin. Children's skin is more susceptible to scalding than adult skin—but no one is immune.

Do not store items over the stove, so that you do not have to reach over burning flames or hot, steaming food. Make sure you never trail electrical cords over flames (such as those for electric hand mixers). If the stove is near a window, remember that curtains can flutter in the breeze right into the hot burner.

All fabric burns, but natural fabrics, such as cotton, linen, and silk, catch fire more easily than synthetics. Wool is the exception to the rule—it burns slowly. Synthetic fibers do not ignite easily but they do melt, which causes deep burns. When natural and synthetic fibers are woven together, they present the most lethal combination of fast-burning fiber and hot, melting material.

Clothing fire victims are four times more likely to die from their injuries than fire victims whose clothes do not ignite or melt. Far more body surface gets burned and, on average, six times as much skin is burned to its full thickness. Clothing fire victims spend an average of twenty-one more days in the hospital than other burn victims.

When you cook, dress comfortably and take care that hanging sleeves, scarves, belts, and ties do not come in contact with burners or the oven. It's best to remove them or tie them back. It's also advisable to tie back long hair.

Not only do aprons protect clothing from spills; they often hold it back from flames.

If you or someone else in the kitchen gets burned, quickly remove any clothing covering the burn and immediately run cold water directly over the area or submerge it in cold water. This literally stops the burning and prevents further thermal injury. Do not rub butter or grease over the burn. If the clothing is on fire, follow the "stop, drop, and roll" advice given in every fire safety course. Use a blanket to extinguish the flames—*not* your hands! Except for the most minor burn, call the doctor or an emergency number. Burns are deceiving and often appear less serious than they are.

Children in the Kitchen

The kitchen is a great place to spend time with your kids, but only if proper safety measures are taken. From a very early age, make sure children associate stoves and ovens with "hot." Do not let them cook anything unattended until you are completely confident of their abilities and good sense. The best age for this may differ from child to child. Many teens are not ready to cook without supervision.

Teach children not to turn the knobs on stoves and ovens unless you are watching them. These are often tempting to young children, and when you are in the kitchen with a toddler or preschooler, be especially aware of how they are occupying themselves. Turn pot handles toward the back of the stove so that youngsters do not pull the pans off the stove, and when possible, use the burners near the rear of the stove for cooking. Do not set hot pots on dish towels on the countertop; a child could yank a trailing piece of the towel and pull the pot over on himself. Take care with hot coffee and the still-hot coffee grounds, which can burn tender young skin more readily than adult skin. Block all electrical outlets in the kitchen with outlet covers. In general, make sure all electrical outlets near the sink and the stove have ground-fault circuit interrupters to prevent shocks.

When to Call the Fire Department

Tragic as it may sound, I have witnessed fires raging out of control that could have been extinguished easily if the fire department had been called sooner. My advice is always to call the fire department, no matter how small or insignificant you think a fire may be. I have never met a firefighter who was angry that he or she was called out for a small fire or an honest false alarm. Prank false alarms are a different story. They are extremely dangerous because they occupy fire apparatus and firefighters who might be urgently needed elsewhere.

Some people seem embarrassed when three engine companies and two ladder companies pull up and the fire turns out to be very small. They tell us that because it was only a "little fire" we did not need to come in full force! But what if the fire had spread and we had had to send for the "rest of the company"? That would waste valuable time.

Keep the number of the fire department posted near all telephones. In some towns and cities, 911 routes calls to the fire department; in others the fire department shares a telephone number and dispatcher with the police; and in some places it has a separate number. Discover how to reach your fire department in a hurry. When you call, be prepared to provide the dispatcher with your name, address, and telephone number, and the nature of the emergency. Do not hang up but wait for acknowledgment of your report. Be sure a babysitter, housekeeper, home health-care worker, or visiting relative or friend knows how to reach the fire department and knows your address and telephone number.

Once you have reported a fire, leave the house. In some cases the fire may be small enough for you to control it with an extinguisher—but remember that a fire can double in size every two to three minutes and the best strategy is to leave the premises. Close the doors behind you but do not lock them. Wait outside for the fire trucks so that you can direct the firefighters to the scene. Finally, make sure your house number is clearly visible from the street.

Firefighter Terms

Backdraft: A backdraft is created when a fire smoldering in a sealed room or building comes into sudden contact with oxygen. The fire "inhales" the oxygen and explodes with a vengeance. Firefighters understandably dread backdrafts because they are incredibly dangerous. This is why they take every precaution when entering a closed room or building.

Chauffeur: The driver of a fire engine in New York is called a chauffeur. His job is to find the fire address and then the nearest hydrant as quickly as possible. He then is responsible for hooking the hose up to the hydrant. During the fire he sees that adequate pressure is maintained to all hose lines.

Cockloft: A cockloft is the area between the ceiling of the attic and the actual roof. If may be unused space where there is a lot of old wood. This area is susceptible to an accelerating fire, and firefighters are wisely wary of entering the cockloft of any building.

Coffin Cut: Firefighters find it necessary to use axes and chainsaws to get into buildings. This may be to gain access or to search for the fire. A coffin cut is made on a flat, internal roof when you are trying to reach a fire under the roof so that you can douse it with water. The size hole cut is usually about the size and shape of a coffin.

Probie: A rookie firefighter who remains on probation for one year after training school.

Red Devil: New York City firefighters call fires that have gained headway the red devil.

Smokehouse: This is the term given to the building used during training school that is filled with smoke and through which the probies have to crawl.

The Rock: This is the nickname New York City firefighters have given the Firefighter Training School.

Truckie: This is NYFD slang for a firefighter assigned to a ladder company. It is the truckies' job to gain access to the fire building, ventilate it, and search for possible victims. Not surprisingly, there is a friendly rivalry between ladder companies and engine companies. Engine members brag that their job, to get water on the fire, is the most important; ladder companies insist theirs is the crucial task. In reality, both jobs are vitally important and all firefighters are dependent on one another, often for their lives.

Turn Out: When an alarm is received, the firefighter on house watch announces which company is responding, at which time firefighters stop whatever they are doing, pull on boots, coats, and helmets, and "turn out" for the fire without delay.

Eating Healthy, Eating Smart

Each recipe in this book is followed by a simple, easy-to-follow nutritional breakdown. It includes the number of calories and amounts of protein (in grams), carbohydrates (in grams), total fat (in grams), saturated fat (in grams), cholesterol (in milligrams), sodium (in milligrams), and fiber (in grams), plus the percentage of calories from fat. Keep in mind that these are very close estimates, meant to provide you with a guideline when you are preparing meals.

As a rule, we all should limit our fat intake to less than 30 percent of our total calories for the day. Some guidelines suggest limiting it to 20 percent. I have designed these recipes so that they easily fall into the first recommendation; many fall into the second. Fifty to 60 percent of our daily diets should be composed of complex carbohydrates (rice, potatoes, bread, fruits, and vegetables). This translates to four or five servings of fruits and vegetables and five or six servings of breads, legumes, potatoes, and grains. These foods also provide much-needed fiber, which has been linked to the prevention of heart disease and some cancers.

Maintaining a Healthy Diet

To ensure that you eat correctly for the best health, I have constructed a set of "Rules to Eat By." They have helped me. I hope they help you too!

- **Start every day with a good breakfast.** As reported in the *American Journal of Clinical Nutrition,* a study of fifty-two moderately obese women showed that those who skipped breakfast lost less weight than those who ate three full meals a day—even though both groups consumed exactly same number of calories. Those who ate breakfast tended to snack less and thus consumed less fat.

  Replace high-fat breakfast foods such as whole eggs, bacon, sausage, and butter- or margarine-spread muffins with whole-grain cereals, fruits, and plain bread. The Turn Out Shake (page 47) is a good, fast breakfast when you are on the run.

- **Eat less as the day goes on.** Studies conducted at the University of Minnesota showed that a single daily 2,000-calorie meal eaten at breakfast time for a week resulted in weight loss; the same number of calories consumed once a day at supper time resulted in weight gain. Follow the old adage of eating breakfast like a king, lunch like a prince, and dinner like a pauper.

- **Eat small, frequent meals.** Try dividing your daily intake into four to six meals. Digestion is easier, and the calories and nutrients are utilized more rapidly and efficiently, so that you tend to store less fat. This also helps stabilize amino acid and glucose levels.

- **Never starve yourself in an attempt to lose weight.** Adjust your caloric intake downward slowly and your level of exercise upward, and make it your goal to lose one or two pounds a week. Starving signals the body to conserve fat and slow down its metabolism. This results in lack of energy and overall poor health. Don't be afraid to eat—but be aware of *what* you eat.

- **Avoid late-night, high-fat snacks.** Just before bed is the worst time for "junk" food. Your metabolism works at half speed while you sleep. If you are hungry late in the evening, try a high-carbohydrate food, such as fruit, and keep the calorie count to 100 or below. High-protein food is nearly as bad as high-fat food. Both tend to inhibit sleep because your body needs to exert considerable energy to burn them. If you do occasionally crave junk food, eat it early in the day.

- **Learn to read food labels.** Thanks to recent laws, food labels now provide a wealth of information about the nutritive value of the food. Ingredients are listed according to weight, from most to least. Labels also list the percentage of fat and saturated fat as well as information on protein, carbohydrates, calories, fiber, sodium, cholesterol and so on.

- **When eating out, always ask how the meal is prepared.** Avoid dishes that are fried, deep-fried, creamed, or served in butter sauce. Look for foods that are broiled, grilled, poached, steamed, and roasted.

- **Learn basic cooking techniques that automatically cut out fat.** Use nonstick pans and grill, broil, or poach foods whenever possible. Poached fish and chicken are wonderful and have no added fats. Trim the fat from meats and poultry and select lean cuts, which are usually labeled "select" or "lean" ("choice" and "prime" cuts are higher in fat). Choose ground meat that has no more than 15 percent fat and be sure to pour off the fat after browning it. Remove the skin from poultry before cooking if possible; it contains most of the fat. Use fresh herbs for flavor instead of oils and high-fat sauces. Replace salt with lemon juice when possible.

- **Learn to cook.** Nothing beats a home-cooked meal. By cooking your own food, you can control the cooking methods and the amounts of fat, sodium, and sugar. You can season food the way you like it. And best of all, you can constantly challenge yourself with new and exciting recipes.

Breakfast

Whole Wheat Orange Muffins

Firefighter John Morris   Makes 12 muffins
Chief 3 Aide
Washington, D.C., Fire Department
Washington, D.C.

Whole wheat muffins are a great way to start the day. They fill you up while providing lots of necessary fiber and B vitamins without a lot of calories and fat.

1 large egg
2 large egg whites
½ cup sugar
⅓ cup canola or other vegetable oil
1 cup fresh orange juice
Grated zest of 2 oranges
1 cup all-purpose flour
1½ cups whole wheat flour
1 teaspoon baking powder
1 teaspoon baking soda
½ teaspoon salt

Preheat the oven to 400°F. Lightly grease or spray a 12-muffin pan or line it with paper muffin wrappers.

In a large bowl, whisk the egg, egg whites, and sugar together, then gradually whisk in the oil, followed by the orange juice and orange zest.

$\mathbb{I}$n another bowl, sift together the flours, baking powder, baking soda, and salt. Add the flour mixture to the liquids and whisk until just barely smooth. Do not overmix. Fill the muffin cups two thirds full.

$\mathbb{B}$ake for 15 to 20 minutes, until the muffins are lightly browned.

NUTRITIONAL CONTENT PER SERVING: (**1 serving** = **1 muffin**)

Calories: 192   Protein: 4 g   Carbohydrates: 30 g   Fat: 7 g   Saturated fat: 1 g

Cholesterol: 35 mg   Sodium: 193 mg   Fiber: 2 g   31 percent calories from fat

Raisin Bran Muffins

Firefighter Paul Schaefer
Station No. 1
Cedar Falls, Iowa

Makes 9 muffins

A lot of guys I know think of raisin bran as a cereal, period. But the combination also makes a great muffin. Bran, the outside shell of whole grains, is an excellent source of fiber. The most common type of bran comes from wheat and is sold in many groceries and supermarkets and in all natural-food stores. Sometimes it's called "unprocessed bran." Oat and rice bran are also readily available.

1¼ cups all-purpose flour
½ cup whole wheat flour
½ cup wheat or oat bran
¼ cup packed light brown sugar
2 teaspoons baking powder
½ teaspoon salt
¾ cup skim milk
1 large egg, beaten
1 large egg white, beaten
¼ cup honey
2 tablespoons canola or other vegetable oil
⅔ cup raisins

Preheat the oven to 425°F. Lightly grease or spray a 9-muffin pan or line it with paper muffin wrappers.

In a medium bowl, combine the flours, bran, brown sugar, baking powder, and salt. Add the milk, egg, egg white, honey, and oil. Mix just until the ingredients are combined and moistened. Do not overmix. Stir in the raisins.

Fill the muffin cups two thirds full and bake for 15 to 20 minutes, until the muffins are lightly browned.

NUTRITIONAL CONTENT PER SERVING: **(1 serving = 1 muffin)**

Calories: 210   Protein: 5 g   Carbohydrates: 41 g   Fat: 4 g   Saturated fat: 1 g

Cholesterol: 24 mg   Sodium: 247 mg   Fiber: 3 g   22 percent calories from fat

Banana Bran Muffins

Firefighter Jennifer Perley
Madbury Volunteer Fire Department
Madbury, New Hampshire

Makes 20 muffins

I guess mornings get pretty cold where Jennifer Perley comes from, and a robust muffin like this would taste awfully good with a cup of strong coffee on any frosty morning—but especially after fighting an early-morning blaze. Using bananas for moisture and sweetness in muffins is a great way to load up on potassium and flavor and to cut back on sugar.

2 large eggs
2 large egg whites
1 cup evaporated skim milk
1 cup unsweetened apple juice
½ cup sugar
½ cup honey
¼ cup canola or other vegetable oil
1 ripe banana, sliced
1 teaspoon ground cinnamon
1½ teaspoons vanilla extract
3 cups crispy bran cereal
1 cup raisins
2½ cups all-purpose flour
1 tablespoon baking soda

Preheat the oven to 400°F. Lightly grease or spray two 10- or 12-muffin pans or line them with paper muffin wrappers. You will only need 20 muffin cups, so fill any unused cups with water during baking.

In a blender or food processor, combine the eggs, egg whites, milk, apple juice, sugar, honey, oil, banana, cinnamon, and vanilla. Blend until smooth.

In a bowl, combine the cereal and raisins and add the blended liquids. Mix well and let stand for 15 minutes to soften the cereal. Sift the flour and baking soda through a wire strainer onto a piece of waxed paper and stir into the cereal mixture. Do not overmix.

Fill the muffin cups two thirds full. Bake for 15 to 20 minutes, until the muffins are lightly browned.

NUTRITIONAL CONTENT PER SERVING: (1 serving = 1 muffin)
Calories: 225   Protein: 6 g   Carbohydrates: 45 g   Fat: 4 g   Saturated fat: 1 g
Cholesterol: 38 mg   Sodium: 327 mg   Fiber: 5 g   16 percent calories from fat

Sweet Potato Cornmeal Muffins

I can't tell you how good for you sweet potatoes are. They top the list of foods rich in beta carotene and are extremely high in fiber. They flavor these muffins by lending their distinctive sweetness, and the pineapple, which also is nice and sweet, gives the muffins wonderful moistness.

1 large sweet potato (about 9 ounces)
1¼ cups all-purpose flour
½ cup yellow cornmeal
¼ cup sugar
2 teaspoons baking powder
½ teaspoon salt
½ teaspoon ground cinnamon
¼ teaspoon grated nutmeg
One 8¼-ounce can crushed unsweetened pineapple, well drained
1 cup evaporated skim milk
3 tablespoons canola or other vegetable oil
1 large egg
2 large egg whites

Preheat the oven to 375°F.

Bake the sweet potato for 45 to 50 minutes, until tender. Let it cool, and when cool enough to handle, scoop out the flesh and discard the skin. Set aside the cooked sweet potato.

Raise the oven temperature to 400°F. Lightly grease or spray a 12-muffin pan or line it with paper muffin wrappers.

In a large bowl, whisk the flour, cornmeal, sugar, baking powder, salt, cinnamon, and nutmeg until smooth. In another bowl, combine the cooked sweet potato, pineapple, milk, oil, egg, and egg whites and whisk well. Pour this mixture into the dry ingredients and whisk just until combined and moistened. Do not overmix.

Fill the muffin cups two thirds full. Bake for 15 to 20 minutes, until golden brown.

NUTRITIONAL CONTENT PER SERVING: (1 serving = 1 muffin)
Calories: 172   Protein: 5 g   Carbohydrates: 29 g   Fat: 4 g   Saturated fat: 1 g
Cholesterol: 18 mg   Sodium: 257 mg   Fiber: 2 g   22 percent calories from fat

Blazin' Banana Date-Nut Muffins

Firefighter Dominick Randazzo
Engine Company 273
New York City Fire Department
Flushing, New York

Makes 12 muffins

Once considered exotic, dates still are a treat to be savored. Their flavor and natural moistness make them perfect for baking, and because they marry so well with nuts, they are often paired with them. If you find dates hard to chop, toss them with a little flour first to reduce the stickiness. These muffins are a powerhouse of vitamins and fruity flavors because, besides dates, they also include bananas and applesauce.

2 large egg whites
⅓ cup low-fat milk
3 ripe bananas, mashed
½ cup unsweetened applesauce
¼ cup packed brown sugar
1½ cups all-purpose flour
½ cup whole wheat flour
1 tablespoon baking powder
1 teaspoon ground cinnamon
½ teaspoon grated nutmeg
½ teaspoon salt
⅓ cup chopped dates
¼ cup chopped walnuts

Preheat the oven to 400°F. Lightly grease or spray a 12-muffin pan or line it with paper muffin wrappers.

In a large bowl, whisk the egg whites, milk, bananas, applesauce, and brown sugar until well combined.

Sift the flours, baking powder, cinnamon, nutmeg, and salt through a wire strainer onto a piece of waxed paper. Whisk—do not beat—the sifted ingredients into the liquid mixture just until moistened. Stir in the dates and walnuts.

Fill the muffin cups two thirds full. Bake for 15 to 20 minutes, until the muffins are lightly browned.

NUTRITIONAL CONTENT PER SERVING: (1 serving = 1 muffin)

Calories: 158   Protein: 3 g   Carbohydrates: 32 g   Fat: 2 g   Saturated fat: 0 g
Cholesterol: 18 mg   Sodium: 261 mg   Fiber: 2 g   14 percent calories from fat

Buttermilk Apple Bran Muffins

Buttermilk is a wonderful ingredient for tenderizing baked goods and adding just a little zing. All buttermilk sold in the supermarkets is low-fat, so you don't have to worry about hidden fat calories. If you don't have buttermilk and want to make these muffins, simply stir a tablespoon of cider vinegar into a cup of low-fat milk for similar results. Like all muffins, these freeze well, so it's no problem to make a batch of twelve even though you want only one or two on any given day.

¾ cup whole wheat flour
½ cup all-purpose flour
1 cup oat bran
⅔ cup packed brown sugar
1 teaspoon baking powder
1 teaspoon baking soda
¼ teaspoon salt
¼ teaspoon grated nutmeg
¼ teaspoon ground cinnamon
1 cup buttermilk or 1 tablespoon vinegar mixed with 1 cup low-fat milk
2 large egg whites
2 tablespoons canola or other vegetable oil
¾ cup peeled and grated tart apple, such as Granny Smith
    (1 small apple)

Preheat the oven to 400°F. Lightly grease or spray a 12-muffin pan or line it with paper muffin wrappers.

In a medium bowl, whisk the flours, oat bran, sugar, baking powder, baking soda, salt, nutmeg, and cinnamon until combined.

In another bowl, whisk the buttermilk, egg whites, and oil until smooth. Whisk the buttermilk mixture into the dry ingredients until just combined and barely moistened. The batter will be slightly stiff. Stir in the grated apple.

Fill the muffin cups two thirds full. Bake for 15 to 20 minutes, until the muffins are lightly browned.

NUTRITIONAL CONTENT PER SERVING: **(1 serving = 1 muffin)**
Calories: 117   Protein: 4 g   Carbohydrates: 22 g   Fat: 3 g   Saturated fat: 0 g
Cholesterol: 7 mg   Sodium: 153 mg   Fiber: 3 g   22 percent calories from fat

Banana Cheese Blintzes

Makes 16 blintzes

A blintz is simply a cheese-filled crepe—and in New York City we love them! I especially like this one because the crepe batter is made with bananas and all the ingredients are whipped together in a flash in the blender or food processor. I got the recipe for the crepes from Chiquita Banana's Spa Chiquita brochure and then devised my own light, low-fat filling. Make sure the bananas are very ripe (nicely speckled on the outside). The crepes can be cooked up to 4 hours ahead, loosely covered, and kept at room temperature. Or they can be cooked up to 2 days ahead of time. If you plan to make them this far ahead, stack them with a piece of waxed paper separating each one and then cover the stack tightly with plastic wrap and refrigerate. The blintzes can be filled up to 2 hours ahead, covered, and held at room temperature.

CREPE BATTER

1½ cups whole wheat pastry flour

2 cups low-fat milk

2 ripe bananas

1 large egg

2 large egg whites

⅛ teaspoon salt

1 tablespoon canola or other vegetable oil

1 teaspoon vanilla extract

¼ teaspoon grated nutmeg

FILLING

1 cup sugarless apricot or blueberry preserves

2 cups nonfat ricotta or cottage cheese

1 tablespoon butter, melted

Confectioners' sugar

In a blender, combine the flour, milk, bananas, egg, egg whites, salt, oil, vanilla, and nutmeg and blend until smooth. Pour the batter into a bowl, cover, and refrigerate for 1 to 2 hours.

Spray an 8-inch nonstick skillet with nonstick cooking spray. Heat the skillet over medium heat until a drop of water dropped onto it sizzles.

Pour ¼ cup of the chilled batter into the skillet and tilt to spread the batter evenly on the bottom. Cook for about 30 seconds, until the underside is golden brown. With a rubber spatula, loosen and turn the crepe (or loosen and flip it). Cook the other side for about 15 seconds, until it is lightly browned and the crepe is cooked through.

Transfer the crepe to a plate and repeat the process with the remaining batter. Make a total of 16 crepes.

Preheat the oven to 350°F. Lightly spray a 10-by-15-inch baking sheet with nonstick cooking spray.

Spread the spotted side of a crepe with 1 tablespoon of preserves, making a circle about 3 inches wide in the center of the crepe. Top with 2 tablespoons of the ricotta or cottage cheese. Fold about 2 inches of the crepe on each side over the filling. Starting with an open edge, roll up the crepe to enclose the filling.

Transfer the filled, rolled blintz to the baking sheet. Repeat the process with the remaining crepes, preserves, and cheese. Drizzle the blintzes with melted butter and bake for about 15 minutes, until the filling is heated through. Sprinkle with confectioners' sugar and serve immediately.

NUTRITIONAL CONTENT PER SERVING: (1 serving = 2 blintzes)

Calories: 217   Protein: 15 g   Carbohydrates: 30 g   Fat: 5 g   Saturated fat: 2 g
Cholesterol: 35 mg   Sodium: 307 mg   Fiber: 4 g   20 percent calories from fat

Firehouse Frittata

Turkey bacon has about half the calories and fat of pork bacon. I mix it with liquid egg substitute, which really cuts down on cholesterol and tastes "like the real thing" when cooked this way. I usually serve this in a crust and call it a quiche, but by baking it without a crust, I omit a lot of fat and unwanted calories—and I can call it a frittata. (Everybody knows firemen don't eat quiche!)

14 slices (about 8 ounces) turkey bacon
1 teaspoon canola or other vegetable oil
1 medium onion, finely chopped
1 clove garlic, minced
2 cups liquid egg substitute
¾ cup skim milk
2 tablespoons chopped fresh parsley
½ teaspoon salt
⅛ teaspoon black pepper
⅛ teaspoon grated nutmeg
2 cups (about 8 ounces) shredded nonfat mozzarella cheese

Preheat the oven to 350°F. Lightly spray a 10-inch round glass pie plate with nonstick cooking spray.

Place the turkey bacon strips on a baking sheet. Bake for 7 to 10 minutes, then turn and bake for 7 to 10 minutes more, until the bacon is crisp. Transfer the bacon to paper towels to drain. When cool, crumble the bacon coarsely. Reduce the oven temperature to 300°F.

In a medium nonstick skillet, heat the oil over medium heat. Add the onion and garlic and cook, covered, for about 5 minutes until the onion is soft.

In medium bowl, whisk together the liquid egg substitute, milk, parsley, salt, pepper, and nutmeg. Stir in the crumbled bacon, mozzarella cheese, and cooked onion and garlic. Pour the mixture into the prepared pie plate.

Place the pie plate in a larger baking dish and transfer to the oven. Add enough hot water to the larger dish to come halfway up the sides of the pie plate. Bake for 50 minutes to 1 hour, until a sharp knife inserted in the center of the frittata comes out clean. Let stand 10 minutes before serving.

NUTRITIONAL CONTENT PER SERVING: Calories: 166   Protein: 20 g   Carbohydrates: 6 g
Fat: 6 g   Saturated fat: 1 g   Cholesterol: 3 mg   Sodium: 841 mg   Fiber: 0 g
27 percent calories from fat

Banana Walnut Power Pancakes

Firefighter Robert Joel

Makes 20 pancakes

Ladder Company 129

New York City Fire Department

Flushing, New York

You may never have considered putting nuts in pancake batter, but then you may not have thought of adding bananas and applesauce either. Friend and fellow firefighter Robert Joel came up with this recipe for a pancake that really packs a wallop in terms of flavor and nutrients. Whenever he makes these at the firehouse, we all hope the alarm doesn't sound until we're done!

1 cup whole wheat flour

1 cup all-purpose flour

1 teaspoon baking soda

3½ cups skim milk

3 large egg whites

1 tablespoon canola or other vegetable oil

1 teaspoon vanilla extract

2 ripe bananas, coarsely chopped

½ cup finely chopped walnuts

2½ cups unsweetened applesauce

In a medium bowl, whisk the flours and baking soda to combine. Add the milk, egg whites, oil, and vanilla, and whisk until barely smooth. Stir in the bananas and walnuts.

Spray a medium nonstick skillet with nonstick cooking spray and heat over medium heat. Ladle the batter onto the skillet, using about ¼ cup of batter for each pancake. When small bubbles appear on the surface of each pancake, turn and cook on the other side until brown. Repeat with the remaining batter. Serve hot with applesauce.

NUTRITIONAL CONTENT PER SERVING: **(1 serving = 2 pancakes)**

Calories: 220   Protein: 11 g   Carbohydrates: 36 g   Fat: 6 g   Saturated fat: 0 g
Cholesterol: 2 mg   Sodium: 146 mg   Fiber: 3 g   23 percent calories from fat

Coffee to Go

Even in the coldest weather you begin to sweat when you reach a working fire—a "signal 10-75" over the dispatcher's radio. But no matter how hot the fire is, once it is extinguished, the frigid winter temperature turns the dripping site to ice. This is true, too, of the firefighters' drenched clothing and equipment.

I remember one cold evening with temperatures in the single digits when we responded to a fire that turned out to be an all-nighter. Because it was such a big fire—a "surround and drown" job with tower ladders pouring rivers of water on a collapsed movie theater's roof—the Red Cross responded with well-stocked coffee wagons. A fellow firefighter and I were soaked by a tower ladder's massive water cannon and our boots filled to the brim with water. We took them off and dumped out the water, not realizing that the water provided some insulation for our feet. When the fire was extinguished and the rest of the firefighters had had their fill of coffee and cocoa and were packing up to head home, my friend and I approached the coffee wagon and asked for thirty cups of coffee and thirty cups of cocoa. How were we going to carry so many cups back to our company, the Red Cross workers wondered? We each raised a steaming cup, drank it, and then, smiling broadly, picked up the remaining fifty-eight cups one by one and poured the hot liquid into our boots. We squished and gurgled as we walked away, but our toes were warm!

Rickster French Toast

Firefighter Richard McCarthy

Serves 3

Ladder Company 129

New York Fire Department

Flushing, New York

Rick is one of the best-liked firefighters in Ladder Company 129. Coming from a traditional firefighting family—his father, now retired, was a high-ranking chief in New York City—Rick arrived in the department after trying his hand as a cook in a seafood restaurant and then doing service as a police officer. Rick often starts his day at the firehouse by making his style of French toast for himself and for the guys who are getting off the night tour.

1 large ripe banana

½ cup skim milk

2 large egg whites

2 tablespoons honey

1 teaspoon ground cinnamon

½ teaspoon vanilla extract

6 slices whole wheat bread

6 tablespoons sugarless fruit preserves

In a blender, combine the banana, milk, egg whites, honey, cinnamon, and vanilla and blend until smooth. Pour into a shallow dish.

Spray a large nonstick skillet with nonstick cooking spray and heat over medium heat.

Dip a slice of bread into the milk mixture and turn to coat both sides. Lay the coated bread in the skillet and cook for about 2 minutes on one side, until golden brown. Turn and cook the other side for about 2 minutes, until golden brown. Remove the French toast from the pan and keep warm. Repeat with the rest of the bread.

Place 2 slices of French toast on each of 3 serving plates. Garnish each with 2 tablespoons of fruit preserves and serve immediately.

NUTRITIONAL CONTENT PER SERVING: **(1 serving = 2 slices French toast with 2 tablespoons fruit spread)**

Calories: 141   Protein: 6 g   Carbohydrates: 28 g   Fat: 1 g   Saturated fat: 0 g

Cholesterol: 2 mg   Sodium: 228 mg   Fiber: 3 g   8 percent calories from fat

Firepower Egg Scramble

Serves 2

This recipe may sound a little strange when you first read it, but once you understand its evolution, you'll be eager to try it. Steak and eggs used to be the athlete's traditional breakfast because of the powerful protein punch the two foods supplied. We know a lot more about cholesterol and fat these days, and the very thought of teaming whole eggs and steak leaves many health-conscious people quivering in their running shoes! I thought about the protein, though, and figured that since most of the protein in eggs is in the whites, I would come up with an equally delicious breakfast that packed just as much protein but very little cholesterol and fat. I coat white-meat chicken with spicy seasoning and scramble the meat plus some vegetables with egg whites or liquid egg substitute. The result is filling and great-tasting. Bear in mind that the main ingredient in liquid egg substitute is egg whites.

3 ounces skinless, boneless chicken breast, cubed
1 tablespoon Cajun seasoning
½ cup thinly sliced fresh mushrooms
½ medium green bell pepper, seeded and finely chopped
½ small onion, minced
8 large egg whites or 1 cup liquid egg substitute

Put the chicken cubes in a bowl and sprinkle with Cajun seasoning. Toss to coat.

Spray a large nonstick skillet with nonstick cooking spray and heat over medium heat. Sauté the chicken for about 4 minutes, turning occasionally, just until firm.

Add the mushrooms, green pepper, and onion and sauté with the chicken for about 3 minutes, until the vegetables soften. Pour the egg whites or egg substitute over the chicken and vegetable mixture. Cook for about 2 minutes, stirring often, until the eggs are barely set or reach desired doneness.

Divide the "scramble" evenly between 2 serving plates and serve immediately.

NUTRITIONAL CONTENT PER SERVING: **Calories: 122   Protein: 21 g**
Carbohydrates: 7 g   Fat: 1 g   Saturated fat: 0 g   Cholesterol: 15 mg
Sodium: 505 mg   Fiber: 2 g   5 percent calories from fat

Grapefruit Vancouver

Here is a fancy breakfast that looks lavish and far more difficult to prepare than it really is. It's very low in fat and makes a wonderful weekend breakfast or brunch dish. It is definitely not firehouse fare, although the recipe was given to me by a friend from Vancouver who has a special fondness for firefighters. Be sure the broiler is preheated and the broiler tray in place or the yogurt will melt before the meringue has a chance to brown.

2 whole grapefruit, cut in half
4 large egg whites, at room temperature
¼ cup sugar
⅛ teaspoon vanilla extract
1 pint hard-frozen vanilla nonfat yogurt

Position the broiler rack 4 to 6 inches from the source of the heat. Preheat the broiler.

Using a sharp knife, carefully cut out and remove the grapefruit pulp, section by section, leaving the membranes intact. Put the pulp in a bowl and set aside. Cut out the membranes to leave 4 empty shells. Spoon the pulp back into each one.

In a separate bowl, combine the egg whites and sugar. Beat until stiff peaks form, then beat in the vanilla. Put ½ cup frozen yogurt on top of each grapefruit half. Mound the egg whites over the yogurt and swirl with the back of a spoon to form small peaks. Set the grapefruit halves on a baking pan and broil for about 1 minute, until the meringue turns golden brown. Serve immediately.

NUTRITIONAL CONTENT PER SERVING: Calories: 199 Protein: 9 g Carbohydrates: 42 g
Fat: 0 g Saturated fat: 0 g Cholesterol: 2 mg Sodium: 119 mg Fiber 2 g
1 percent calories from fat

Turn Out Shake

Serves 4

In firehouse parlance, "turn out" means that an alarm has been received and the firefighter on house watch will announce over the loudspeaker which company is responding. When we hear the announcement, we drop everything, pull on boots, coats, and helmets, and turn out with utmost speed. This shake is an excellent source of quick carbohydrates for energy on those days when you don't have time to prepare breakfast but must "turn out" to start the day. It helps to have the ingredients chilled before blending.

¾ cup chilled fresh orange juice
1 ripe banana, cut into chunks
1 chilled 16-ounce can unsweetened pineapple chunks in juice,
    undrained
1 cup chilled sliced strawberries

In a blender, combine the orange juice, banana, pineapple chunks with their juice, and strawberries. Blend until smooth. Divide among 4 tall glasses and serve.

NUTRITIONAL CONTENT PER SERVING: Calories: 248 Protein: 3 g
Carbohydrates: 63 g Fat: 1 g Saturated fat: 0 g Cholesterol: 0 mg
Sodium: 4 mg Fiber: 5 g 3 percent calories from fat

Salads

Firehouse Waldorf Salad

Serves 4

Everyone who lives in New York has heard of the Waldorf-Astoria Hotel. Years ago the chef there created a salad that had apples and walnuts in it and was dressed with a rich, creamy mayonnaise-based dressing. It was so good, it quickly became an American classic. I substitute a yogurt-honey dressing for the mayonnaise, which makes this version much lighter—and it tastes terrific.

½ cup plain low-fat yogurt
2 tablespoons honey
2 tart apples (such as Granny Smith), cored, peeled, and chopped
2 stalks celery, chopped
1 cup seedless red or green grapes
Lettuce leaves
⅓ cup chopped walnuts

In a medium bowl, stir together the yogurt and honey. Add the apples, celery, and grapes and mix gently.

Place a few lettuce leaves on each of 4 plates. Divide the salad evenly among the plates and sprinkle with walnuts.

NUTRITIONAL CONTENT PER SERVING: Calories: 183   Protein: 4 g
Carbohydrates: 31 g   Fat: 7 g   Saturated fat: 1 g   Cholesterol: 2 mg
Sodium: 42 mg   Fiber: 3 g   30 percent calories from fat

Tomato-Oregano Salad Dressing

Serves 8

Instead of relying on fat (oil) for body in this dressing, I use pureed vegetables for great consistency. Be sure the tomatoes are well drained. If you want to use summer tomatoes from your garden, go right ahead. The dressing may be a little thinner, but the flavor will superb. I particularly like this spooned over a mixture of red leaf lettuce, arugula, and radicchio and tossed with sliced red peppers and zucchini. But it would be equally good tossed with leaf or Boston lettuce.

One 6-ounce can peeled Italian tomatoes in juice, drained
3 tablespoons red wine vinegar
1 teaspoon dried oregano
1 teaspoon honey
1 clove garlic, crushed through a press
¼ teaspoon salt
¼ teaspoon black pepper

In a blender, process all of the ingredients until smooth. Serve as a salad dressing immediately or refrigerate in a tightly lidded glass jar or plastic container for up to 3 days.

NUTRITIONAL CONTENT PER TABLESPOON: **Calories: 10   Protein: 0 g**
Carbohydrates: 3 g   Fat: 0 g   Saturated fat: 0 g   Cholesterol: 0 mg
Sodium: 116 mg   Fiber: 0 g   6 percent calories from fat

Cucumber-Cumin Salad Dressing

Serves 8

The blender is great for making quick salad dressings. This one, with its yogurt base, is creamy and coolly refreshing without being rich or overloaded with fat. I like it spooned over salads of mixed lettuces or sliced tomatoes (the cucumber flavor really shines). It's also good as a dip for vegetables.

1 cup plain low-fat yogurt
1 medium cucumber, peeled, seeded, and cut into chunks
2 scallions, both white and green parts, chopped
1 clove garlic, crushed through a press
1 teaspoon ground cumin
½ teaspoon salt
¼ teaspoon black pepper

In a blender, process all of the ingredients until smooth. Serve as a salad dressing immediately or refrigerate in a tightly lidded glass jar or plastic container for up to 3 days.

NUTRITIONAL CONTENT PER TABLESPOON: **Calories: 28   Protein: 2 g**
Carbohydrates: 4 g   Fat: 1 g   Saturated fat: 0 g   Cholesterol: 2 mg
Sodium: 157 mg   Fiber: 1 g   18 percent calories from fat

The Clean Plate Club

A fellow firefighter who works in the South Bronx told me about a newly appointed lieutenant who, soon after coming on duty in the firehouse, reprimanded the cooks about the cleanliness of the kitchen. "Would you eat off this table?" he asked, ordering them to clean up before he stormed back to his office. The offended veterans—tough firefighters used to battling fires in one of the city's roughest neighborhoods—decided to teach this "johnny" a lesson and, as always, have a good laugh.

When the "chow's on" call came over the loudspeaker that evening, the lieutenant entered the kitchen. There he saw eleven firefighters sitting around the table. In the center were dishes of sliced meat, boiled potatoes, and peas and carrots, all filling the kitchen with delicious aromas. Twelve place settings were neatly laid out, but instead of plates there were twelve circles chalked on the table. Without batting an eye, the cook dished some food into the circle in front of the lieutenant, and every firefighter followed suit, serving himself and eating the food directly off the table. It didn't take long for the lieutenant to catch on to the gag, especially when everyone burst out laughing, and he never complained about the cleanliness of the kitchen again.

Chinese Cabbage Slaw

Firefighter Doug Wetmore
Engine Station 1
Westminster Fire Department
Westminster, California

Serves 6

A lot of the best cooks in California are influenced by Asian cooking, and Firefighter Doug Wetmore is obviously no exception. When I tried this recipe, I really liked the sesame flavor and the crunch provided by the crushed noodles. By the way, ½ ounce of dried noodles is the amount in one package of ramen or similar noodle soup mix. Japanese-style soy sauce is commonly sold in the United States (Kikkoman is one popular brand) and is slightly less salty than Chinese-style soy sauce, also sold here. However, don't worry too much about the soy sauce—use a brand you particularly like. Napa or Chinese cabbage grows in elongated pale green heads and is also called bok choy.

2 tablespoons sesame seeds
½ head (about ¾ pound) Napa or Chinese cabbage, thinly sliced
5 to 6 scallions, both white and green parts, chopped
2 large carrots, shredded
¼ cup rice or white vinegar
⅓ cup unsweetened pineapple juice
2 cloves garlic, crushed through a press
2 tablespoons sugar
1 teaspoon salt
½ teaspoon black pepper
2 tablespoons dark sesame oil
½ ounce uncooked Asian rice noodles, crushed

In a heavy skillet, toast the sesame seeds over medium heat, stirring constantly, for 2 to 3 minutes, until golden brown. Immediately transfer the sesame seeds to a plate to cool.

In a large bowl, combine the cabbage, scallions, and carrots.

In a small bowl, whisk together the vinegar, pineapple juice, garlic, sugar, salt, and pepper. Gradually whisk in the sesame oil.

Pour the dressing over the cabbage mixture, add the sesame seeds, and toss well. Cover and refrigerate for 1 hour before serving. Just before serving, add the crushed noodles and toss. Serve chilled.

NUTRITIONAL CONTENT PER SERVING: **Calories: 347   Protein: 8 g**
Carbohydrates: 49 g   Fat: 16 g   Saturated fat: 2 g   Cholesterol: 0 mg   Sodium: 976 mg
Fiber: 7 g   38 percent calories from fat

Tropical Chicken Salad

Because I am often asked by personal fitness clients and firefighter friends for good ideas for replacing the fatty lunch meats often found in salads and sandwiches, I am including this recipe for a chicken salad. The mayonnaise commonly found in chicken salad is replaced here with a blended mixture of bananas and yogurt. Terrific served on lettuce leaves and garnished with fresh fruit, this salad also tastes good between two slices of whole wheat bread as a sandwich. You could substitute leftover roast chicken for the poached chicken. Be sure to take off any skin, which is the fat-laden culprit when it comes to poultry. I adapted this recipe from the Spa Chiquita brochure.

6 chicken breast halves, bone in and skin on
1 small onion, chopped
Salt
2 black peppercorns
3 ripe bananas, cut in chunks
2 tablespoons finely chopped garlic
¾ cup plain nonfat yogurt
1 tablespoon honey
2 teaspoons fresh lemon juice
Lettuce leaves
Red seedless grapes
Orange sections

In a large saucepan filled with 2 quarts of water, bring the chicken, onion, a pinch of salt, and the peppercorns to a simmer over low heat. Cook for about 25 minutes.

Remove the pan from the heat and let it stand for 30 minutes. Using a slotted spoon, lift the chicken from the cooled broth. Remove and discard the skin and bone. Cut the poached chicken into ¾-inch pieces. Put the pieces in a bowl and refrigerate for at least 30 minutes to cool completely.

In a blender or food processor, combine the bananas, garlic, yogurt, honey, lemon juice, and ¼ teaspoon of salt and blend until creamy. Spoon the "mayonnaise" into the bowl holding the chicken and toss to distribute it evenly. Cover and refrigerate for at least 1 hour.

To serve, arrange a few lettuce leaves on each serving plate, mound the salad on top of the lettuce, and garnish each plate with grapes and orange sections.

NUTRITIONAL CONTENT PER SERVING: **Calories: 224   Protein: 29 g Carbohydrates: 20 g   Fat: 3 g   Saturated fat: 1 g   Cholesterol: 74 mg Sodium: 175 mg   Fiber: 1 g   14 percent calories from fat**

Truckie Taco Salad

Firefighter Richard Brandt
Westminster Fire Department
Westminster, California

Serves 10

Rich used to be a firefighter in New York, and when he moved to California, he joined a fire department there. He was featured in a firefighter "hunk" calendar soon after he moved, which didn't surprise anyone back home because this top-notch softball player had done some modeling in New York. As much as he loves the California lifestyle, Rich admits that he misses the brotherhood of New York City firefighters. Luckily for his new brothers in Westminster, Rich brought his cooking talents with him when he moved west. This salad is a winner.

2½ pounds ground turkey
1 large onion, chopped
¼ cup chili powder, or more to taste
1 tablespoon dried oregano
1 teaspoon ground cumin
One 12-ounce can pitted olives, drained, rinsed, and sliced into slivers
One 28-ounce can kidney beans, drained and rinsed
One 16-ounce can garbanzo beans, drained and rinsed
Two 16-ounce cans pinto beans with jalapeños, drained and rinsed
2 medium tomatoes, diced
2 heads iceberg lettuce, washed and torn into bite-sized pieces
2 cups (about 8 ounces) shredded low-fat, low-sodium Cheddar cheese
8 ounces baked tortilla chips, coarsely crushed

2 cups nonfat mayonnaise

½ cup prepared taco sauce

1 teaspoon hot red pepper sauce, or to taste

In a large nonstick skillet, cook the onions over medium heat until soft and translucent. Add the ground turkey and cook for about 7 minutes, until the turkey loses its pink color. Use a wooden spoon to break the meat apart while it cooks. Carefully drain off any liquid, then stir in the chili powder, oregano, cumin, and salt and cook for 1 minute. Add the olives, kidney beans, garbanzos, and pinto beans and mix well. Stir in the tomatoes.

In a large serving bowl, combine the lettuce, cheese, and chips. Add the turkey mixture and toss well.

In a small bowl, combine the mayonnaise, taco sauce, and hot red pepper sauce. Pass the dressing at the table with the salad.

NUTRITIONAL CONTENT PER SERVING: **Calories: 503   Protein: 36 g**
Carbohydrates: 53 g   Fat: 16 g   Saturated fat: 4 g   Cholesterol: 74 mg
Sodium: 1,454 mg   Fiber: 12 g   29 percent calories from fat

Shrimp and Spinach Salad

Firefighter Gene Tambascio   Serves 6
Fire Station 7
Phoenix Fire Department
Phoenix, Arizona

This is a filling, healthful salad that is especially good in the warm weather months. Shrimp is wonderful mixed with the spinach and rice, but crabmeat is equally good if you prefer. You can buy shrimp cooked and peeled or buy them in the shell and cook and peel them yourself to save money. Buy about 1¾ pounds of medium-sized shrimp in the shell for a pound of shelled shrimp. Cook them in boiling water for 2 to 3 minutes, until the shells turn pink. Let cool, then peel off the shells with your fingers. Using a sharp knife, cut the black vein from the inside of the shrimp as you split each one in half lengthwise.

1 pound fresh spinach
1 cup cooked rice
1 cup (about 4 ounces) shredded part-skim mozzarella cheese
⅓ cup (about 4 ounces) sunflower seeds
1 pound cooked and peeled shrimp, halved lengthwise
½ cup nonfat Italian dressing

Wash the spinach thoroughly and remove the stems. Drain and place in a large bowl.

Add the cooked rice, cheese, sunflower seeds, and shrimp. Mix well. Cover and refrigerate until chilled. Just before serving, add the dressing and toss thoroughly.

NUTRITIONAL CONTENT PER SERVING: **Calories: 381   Protein: 26 g Carbohydrates: 52 g   Fat: 1 g   Saturated fat: 1 g   Cholesterol: 34 mg Sodium: 856 mg   Fiber: 5 g   18 percent calories from fat**

Southwest Bean Salad

Captain John Lusson
Fire Station 5
Phoenix Fire Department
Phoenix, Arizona

Serves 8

This is a variation on three-bean salad with a few more beans than usual. Firefighter John Lusson from Arizona sent it to me, and the influence of his native Southwest is apparent from the addition of kidney beans, sprouts, and green pepper.

4 ounces green beans, fresh or frozen, cut in 1-inch pieces (about ¾ cup)
4 ounces baby lima beans, fresh or frozen (about ¾ cup)
4 ounces yellow wax beans, fresh or frozen, cut in 1-inch pieces
    (about ¾ cup)
One 8-ounce can red kidney beans, drained
2 cups fresh bean sprouts
1 large green bell pepper, seeded and finely chopped
1 small red onion, finely chopped
1 tablespoon sugar
2 tablespoons red wine vinegar
2 tablespoons tomato paste
1 clove garlic, minced
½ teaspoon salt
¼ teaspoon black pepper
6 tablespoons canola or other vegetable oil

If using fresh green, lima, or wax beans, fit a steamer with a basket and steam the beans for about 5 minutes, just until tender. Transfer to a large bowl. If using frozen beans, thaw the beans and put them in the bowl. Add the kidney beans, sprouts, green pepper, and onion and mix.

In a separate bowl, whisk the sugar, vinegar, tomato paste, garlic, salt, and pepper. Gradually whisk in the oil. Pour the dressing over the salad. Cover and refrigerate for at least 4 hours before serving. Serve chilled or at room temperature.

NUTRITIONAL CONTENT PER SERVING: **Calories: 141** **Protein: 5 g**
Carbohydrates: 22 g **Fat: 4 g** **Saturated fat: 1 g** **Cholesterol: 0 mg**
Sodium: 172 mg **Fiber: 5 g** **27 percent calories from fat**

Lexington Avenue Seafood Salad

Firefighter James Moore
Engine Company 8
New York City Fire Department
New York, New York

Serves 4

Jim is with Engine Company 8 in the heart of Manhattan, and so we named this seafood salad after one of that borough's best-known avenues. The company has adopted a Dalmatian mascot whose name is—what else?—Highrise. As a former competitive bodybuilder, Jim knows a lot about healthful eating, and this light salad is as good for you as it is good-tasting. Jim hasn't competed in a number of years, but in 1983 he won the Eastern American Championship and in 1982 the New York Metropolitan Bodybuilding Championship. He's still in great shape.

1 cup cooked baby shrimp
1 cup fresh cooked crabmeat, picked over to remove cartilage
1 cup cooked green peas
½ cup chopped celery
½ medium cucumber, peeled and sliced
2 tablespoons minced onion
½ cup low-fat Thousand Island dressing
¼ cup plain nonfat yogurt
1 tablespoon prepared horseradish
1 teaspoon fresh lemon juice

¼ teaspoon dried marjoram

¼ teaspoon black pepper

Lettuce leaves

In a serving bowl, combine the shrimp, crabmeat, peas, celery, cucumber and onion.

In a small bowl, combine the salad dressing, yogurt, horseradish, lemon juice, marjoram, and pepper. Pour the dressing over the salad and toss.

Place a few lettuce leaves on each of 4 serving plates. Divide the salad evenly among them and serve immediately.

NUTRITIONAL CONTENT PER SERVING: **Calories: 120   Protein: 12 g   Carbohydrates: 15 g   Fat: 2 g   Saturated fat: 1 g   Cholesterol: 47 mg   Sodium: 309 mg   Fiber: 2 g   15 percent calories from fat**

South Bronx Turkey Salad

Serves 8

I grew up in the Bronx, which was then and remains today one of the most ethnically diverse areas of New York City. When I was a kid, the South Bronx in particular was a heavy fire-duty area, and to this day I hear veterans talking about the 1960s and '70s when ten thousand runs (alarms) a year were normal and the department lost ten or fifteen firefighters a year. Most of the burned-out buildings in the South Bronx have been leveled by now, and the area is experiencing something of a comeback, but it is still the busiest fire-duty area in the city. I named this salad after the South Bronx because it's a filling mixture that hits the spot after a hard tour of duty. I suggest using leftover turkey breast, but if you want to buy turkey at the deli, ask for thick slices of real turkey—not pressed turkey roll.

4 cups coarsely chopped cooked turkey
2 cups cooked brown rice
2 medium tomatoes, diced
1 medium green bell pepper, seeded and finely chopped
1 medium red or yellow bell pepper, seeded and finely chopped
¼ cup chopped canned green chiles, drained
¼ cup roughly chopped oil-packed sun-dried tomatoes
½ cup plain nonfat yogurt
2 cloves garlic, crushed through a press
1 tablespoon olive oil
1½ teaspoons chili powder
½ teaspoon ground cumin
¼ teaspoon salt

In a large salad bowl, combine the turkey, rice, tomatoes, peppers, chiles, and sun-dried tomatoes and toss well.

In a small bowl, combine the yogurt, garlic, oil, chili powder, cumin, and salt and stir until well blended.

Just before serving, pour the dressing over the salad and toss well.

NUTRITIONAL CONTENT PER SERVING: **Calories: 222 Protein: 24 g Carbohydrates: 18 g Fat: 6 g Saturated fat: 2 g Cholesterol: 53 mg Sodium: 75 mg Fiber: 2 g 25 percent calories from fat**

Margo's Mushroom Salad

Firefighter Margo Taylor
Metro-Dade Fire Department
Miami, Florida

Serves 8

This light, refreshing salad comes from a "firefem" with a fire company in sunny South Florida. The clam juice gives it a distinctive, unexpected flavor. I loved it the first time I tried it.

⅓ cup bottled clam juice
3 tablespoons balsamic vinegar
1½ teaspoons olive oil
¼ teaspoon dried tarragon
½ teaspoon salt
½ teaspoon black pepper
10 ounces fresh mushrooms, thinly sliced
1 red onion, thinly sliced
1 head Boston lettuce, washed and torn into bite-sized pieces
1 medium tomato, cut into wedges

In a mixing bowl, whisk the clam juice, balsamic vinegar, oil, tarragon, salt, and pepper. Add the mushrooms and red onion. Cover and refrigerate until well chilled.

Put the lettuce in a large salad bowl; pour the mushroom mixture over the lettuce and toss. Garnish with tomato wedges and serve.

NUTRITIONAL CONTENT PER SERVING: **Calories: 31**   **Protein: 2 g**
Carbohydrates: 5 g   **Fat: 1 g**   **Saturated fat: 0 g**   **Cholesterol: 0 mg**
Sodium: 157 mg   **Fiber: 1 g**   **29 percent calories from fat**

 The Healthy Firehouse Cookbook

Bibb Lettuce with Honey-Mustard Dressing

Firefighter Joseph Aquino and Debbie Aquino

Engine Company 42

New York City Fire Department

Bronx, New York (Retired to Montana)

Serves 6

When you make creamy dressings using low-fat yogurt and mayonnaise, you get the richness without the calories and fat. This is a simple recipe for a Bibb lettuce salad that is a wonderful accompaniment with grilled fish or chicken. You could also use Boston lettuce or any buttery green.

¾ cup plain low-fat yogurt

¼ cup nonfat mayonnaise

2 tablespoons honey

2 tablespoons Dijon mustard

1 tablespoon poppy seeds

⅛ teaspoon black pepper

2 heads Bibb lettuce, washed and torn into bite-sized pieces

2 tablespoons chopped fresh chives

In a small bowl, combine the yogurt, mayonnaise, honey, mustard, poppy seeds, and pepper. Cover and refrigerate until ready to serve.

Arrange the lettuce on 6 chilled serving plates. Drizzle with the dressing, sprinkle with the chives, and serve immediately.

NUTRITIONAL CONTENT PER SERVING: **Calories: 67** Protein: 3 g

Carbohydrates: 12 g Fat: 2 g **Saturated fat: 0 g** Cholesterol: 2 mg

Sodium: 203 mg Fiber: 0 g **19 percent calories from fat**

Greek Salad with Dilled Yogurt Dressing

Firefighter Joseph Aquino and Debbie Aquino

Engine Company 42

New York City Fire Department

Bronx, New York (Retired to Montana)

Serves 8

This is not your usual Greek salad with black olives and feta cheese, but it qualifies because of the combination of lettuce, cucumbers, tomatoes, and red onion. What makes it extra special is the low-fat creamy dill dressing. Be sure to use fresh dill—it makes a world of difference in the flavor and is available in supermarkets from coast to coast.

1 cup plain low-fat yogurt

1 scallion, finely chopped

2 tablespoons chopped fresh dill

1 tablespoon nonfat mayonnaise

1 tablespoon skim milk

¼ teaspoon salt

¼ teaspoon black pepper

1 head romaine lettuce, washed and torn into bite-sized pieces

1 medium zucchini, scrubbed and thinly sliced

1 medium cucumber, peeled and thinly sliced

1 large ripe tomato, cut into wedges

1 small red onion, thinly sliced

In a small bowl, combine the yogurt, scallion, dill, mayonnaise, milk, salt, and pepper and stir until smooth. Cover and refrigerate until ready to serve.

In a large salad bowl, toss the lettuce, zucchini, cucumber, tomato, and onion. Drizzle with the salad dressing and toss again. Serve immediately.

NUTRITIONAL CONTENT PER SERVING: **Calories: 52   Protein: 4 g**
Carbohydrates: 9 g   Fat: 1 g   Saturated fat: 0 g   Cholesterol: 2 mg
Sodium: 120 mg   Fiber 0 g   13 percent calories from fat

Soups, Stews, and Chilies

Easy-Does-It Clam Chowder

Firefighter Jim Lyons   Serves 10
Company 3
Glastonbury Fire Department
Glastonbury, Connecticut

This is New England–style clam chowder contributed by a firefighter from Connecticut. A little farther south, in New York, we make chowder with tomatoes, but where Jim comes from it is made from a milky base that often includes cream. There's no cream in this chowder, just skim milk thickened with cornstarch. The Canadian bacon adds great flavor and not a lot of fat. Ditto for the melted butter.

2 ounces Canadian bacon, chopped (about ½ cup)
1 onion, diced
2 dozen large clams, shucked, juice reserved, and chopped
2 medium boiling potatoes, peeled and cut into ½-inch cubes
½ cup bottled clam juice
¼ cup cornstarch
3 cups skim milk
1 teaspoon dried thyme
½ teaspoon dried dill
½ teaspoon dried tarragon
¼ teaspoon salt
½ teaspoon black pepper
1 tablespoon melted butter

Spray a large nonstick skillet with nonstick cooking spray and set over medium heat. Cook the bacon and onion for about 5 minutes, until the onion is translucent.

Transfer the bacon and onion to a large saucepan and add the clams with their juice, the potatoes, and the bottled clam juice. Bring to a simmer and cook over low heat for 10 minutes.

In a separate bowl, whisk the cornstarch with the milk. Gradually whisk the thickened milk into the clam mixture. Add the thyme, dill, tarragon, salt, and pepper. Simmer the chowder for 10 more minutes, stirring occasionally and being careful not to let the chowder boil.

Just before serving, stir in the melted butter. Serve hot.

NUTRITIONAL CONTENT PER SERVING: **Calories: 120 Protein: 6 g Carbohydrates: 19 g Fat: 2 g Saturated fat: 1 g Cholesterol: 10 mg Sodium: 214 mg Fiber: 1 g 15 percent calories from fat**

Chicken Vegetable Soup Stew

Firefighter Kenneth Coffey

Serves 10

Ladder Company 129

New York City Fire Department

Flushing, New York (Retired)

Kenny and I go way back. We met at the firehouse where I was assigned after the Fire Academy and both transferred to Ladder Company 129 at the same time. We had a great time until one night when we both nearly lost our lives. We were called to a three-alarm fire at a row of houses. When we arrived, we immediately knew we had a "job"—firefighter lingo for a working fire. Kenny raced upstairs while I searched the ground flour. He was met at the top of the stairs by a "red devil," a fire that has gained tremendous headway very quickly. This one flared up, creating so much air pressure that Kenny was literally blown back down the stairway. I met him at the bottom when it was suddenly apparent we were both trapped in the stairwell by the fire. No escape! Luckily, our engine company had hoses in place by then and was able to quench the fire sufficiently so that we could leave the building. Ken sustained a career-ending knee injury and is missed by all of us. We especially miss his cooking, which was always health-oriented. I am pleased he contributed this easy, nutritious soup. If you prefer, use canned kidney beans instead of dried. Figure on about 2½ cups of drained canned beans for this recipe.

1 cup dried kidney beans, rinsed

3¾ cups chicken broth, preferably homemade (page 110), or canned
   low-sodium broth

One 14½-ounce can stewed tomatoes

5 cups water

½ cup barley

½ cup dried split peas, rinsed

1 pound carrots, sliced ½ inch thick

6 stalks celery, sliced ½ inch thick

1 large onion, chopped

2 cloves garlic, finely chopped

3 bay leaves

½ teaspoon dried thyme

1 teaspoon black pepper

1 pound skinless, boneless chicken breasts, cut into 1-inch cubes

1 green or red bell pepper, seeded and finely chopped

½ pound green beans, cut into ½-inch pieces

Put the kidney beans in a medium saucepan and add enough cold water to cover by 2 inches. Bring to a boil over high heat. Cook for 2 minutes. Remove from the heat, cover, and let stand for 1 hour. Or, in a medium bowl, soak the beans in 2 quarts of water at room temperature overnight. Drain completely.

In a large soup pot, combine the chicken broth, stewed tomatoes, 5 cups water, soaked kidney beans, barley, split peas, carrots, celery, onion, garlic, bay leaves, thyme, and black pepper. Bring the mixture to a boil over high heat, reduce the heat to low, and simmer for about 2 hours, until the beans and barley are tender.

Add the chicken, bell pepper, and green beans and continue to cook for about 10 minutes, until the chicken is firm. Remove the bay leaves from the soup and serve hot.

NUTRITIONAL CONTENT PER SERVING: **Calories: 259   Protein: 22 g**
Carbohydrates: 39 g   Fat: 3 g   Saturated fat: 1 g   Cholesterol: 29 mg
Sodium: 173 mg   Fiber: 11 g   9 percent calories from fat

Hearty Vegetable-Beef Barley Soup

Chief John Settle
Fredonia Fire Department
Fredonia, Kansas

Serves 12

They know their beef in Kansas, where John comes from. This soup takes advantage of very lean ground beef, which is not particularly high in anything except protein and good flavor.

1 pound lean ground sirloin (90 percent lean)
½ cup chopped onion
2 medium carrots, chopped
2 cloves garlic, chopped
4½ cups beef broth, preferably homemade (page 112), or canned
    low-sodium broth
1 cup barley
One 6-ounce can tomato paste
2 tablespoons chopped fresh parsley
½ teaspoon salt
½ teaspoon black pepper
2 cups fresh or thawed frozen corn kernels
5 ounces green beans, trimmed and cut into 1-inch lengths
1 cup fresh or thawed frozen peas

In a large nonstick skillet, cook the ground sirloin, onion, carrots, and garlic over medium-high heat for about 5 minutes, stirring often, until the meat has lost its pink color.

Drain off any fat and transfer the mixture to a large soup pot. Stir in the beef broth, barley, tomato paste, parsley, salt, and pepper. Bring to a boil over high heat. Reduce the heat to low and simmer, partially covered, for about 2 hours, until the barley is tender.

Add the corn, green beans, and peas and cook for about 15 minutes, until the beans are tender. Serve hot.

NUTRITIONAL CONTENT PER SERVING: **Calories: 178   Protein: 12 g**
Carbohydrates: 31 g   Fat: 2 g   Saturated fat: 1 g   Cholesterol: 16 mg
Sodium: 570 mg   Fiber: 6 g   10 percent calories from fat

Three-Decade Tortellini Soup

Firefighter Joseph Laterza
Ladder Company 129
New York City Fire Department
Flushing, New York

Serves 12

Joe and I went through probationary firefighters school back in 1979. He was first assigned to Engine Company 40 in Manhattan and later transferred to my company in Queens. He's a terrific athlete and has won a silver medal for the 1,600-meter relay and bronze medals for the 200- and 400-meter relays at the Police/Fire World Games. He also is a great cook who leans toward Italian food prepared healthfully. A good example of his abilities, this soup has gotten the two of us through many cold winter afternoons.

Two 3-pound chickens, rinsed and cut into pieces, or 5 pounds chicken
    parts such as backs and wings
1 large onion, diced
2 pounds carrots, chopped
2 bunches celery with leaves, sliced
4 cloves garlic, finely chopped
1 bunch fresh parsley, chopped
1 teaspoon salt
½ teaspoon black pepper
3 pounds cheese-filled tortellini
Freshly grated Parmesan cheese

Put the chicken, onion, carrots, celery, garlic, and parsley into a large pot and add enough cold water to cover by 2 inches. Bring to a boil over high heat; skim off any foam that rises to the surface.

If you are using cut up chickens, reduce the heat to medium-low and cook for about 1 hour, until the chicken is tender. If you are using chicken parts, cook for about 3 hours. When the chicken is cooked, remove it from the broth with tongs. Refrigerate the chicken and reserve for another use. Continue simmering the broth for 30 minutes more. Season with salt and pepper.

Meanwhile, bring a pot of lightly salted water to a boil, add the tortellini, and cook for 10 minutes, until tender. Drain well. Spoon the hot tortellini into soup bowls and ladle the broth and vegetables on top. Sprinkle with grated cheese and serve hot.

NUTRITIONAL CONTENT PER SERVING: **Calories: 516   Protein: 11 g**
Carbohydrates: 55 g   Fat: 14 g   Saturated fat: 5 g   Cholesterol: 199 mg
Sodium: 541 mg   Fiber: 7 g   25 percent calories from fat

Lentil Soup

Firefighter Jeffrey L. Pickover
Coral Gables Fire Department
Coral Gables, Florida

Serves 12

This soup is so filling, it stands on its own as a full meal. It has lentils and brown rice for a good protein count and lots of flavor. Like many soups, this one is almost better eaten the day after it's made.

2 tablespoons canola or other vegetable oil
1 large white or yellow onion, chopped
1 pound carrots, chopped
1 large green bell pepper, seeded and chopped
1 clove garlic, finely chopped
One 14½-ounce can Cajun-style stewed tomatoes or other spicy
    stewed tomatoes
10 cups water
Two 10-ounce packages frozen chopped spinach, thawed and
    squeezed dry
1½ cups dried lentils, rinsed
1 cup brown rice
1 teaspoon dried Italian herb seasoning
½ teaspoon salt
¼ teaspoon black pepper

In a large soup pot, heat the oil over medium heat. Add the onion, carrots, green pepper, and garlic; cover and cook for 5 to 6 minutes, until the vegetables soften.

Stir in the stewed tomatoes and cook for 5 minutes. Stir in the water, spinach, lentils, brown rice, herb seasoning, salt, and pepper. Bring the mixture to a boil and then reduce the heat to low. Cover partially and simmer for about 1 hour, stirring occasionally, until the lentils are very tender. Serve hot.

NUTRITIONAL CONTENT PER SERVING: **Calories: 271** **Protein: 14 g**
Carbohydrates: 48 g **Fat: 4 g** **Saturated fat: 0 g** **Cholesterol: 0 mg**
Sodium: 175 mg **Fiber: 9 g** **12 percent calories from fat**

Spare Change Lentil Soup

Firefighter Kevin Rooney   Serves 6
Engine Company 11
Anne Arundel County Fire Department
Anne Arundel County, Maryland

This is one of the most frugal recipes in the book and illustrates how you can make a good meal with just a few ingredients that most people have on hand. If you don't keep lentils in the cupboard as a matter of course, perhaps you should consider doing so. They keep well in a dark, cool place for several months. They are highly nutritious and, like split peas, are dried legumes that do not require presoaking.

continued

5 cups chicken broth, preferably homemade (page 110), or canned low-
    sodium broth
1 cup dried lentils, rinsed
2 large onions, cut into strips
½ teaspoon salt
¼ teaspoon black pepper
¾ cup chopped fresh parsley

In a large soup pot, combine all the ingredients except the parsley and bring to a boil over medium-high heat. Reduce the heat to low and simmer, partially covered, for about 1½ hours, until the soup thickens and the lentils are tender. Stir in the parsley and simmer for about 5 minutes more before serving. Serve hot.

NUTRITIONAL CONTENT PER SERVING: **Calories: 212   Protein: 16 g**
Carbohydrates: 36 g   Fat: 1 g   Saturated fat: 0 g   Cholesterol: 1 mg
Sodium: 1,124 mg   Fiber: 7 g   6 percent calories from fat

Backdraft Stew

Serves 8

A backdraft is created when a fire smoldering in a sealed room or building comes into sudden contact with oxygen, which the fire actually inhales, causing it to explode in a fury. Firefighters understandably dread backdrafts—which are incredibly dangerous—and take every precaution when entering a closed room or building. I named this stew "backdraft" because the two peppers give it a little fire, particularly the cayenne. Reduce the amount to prevent your own personal backdraft, if you prefer.

4½ cups water

1 tablespoon canola or other vegetable oil

½ teaspoon salt

2 cups brown rice

1 pound ground turkey

1 small onion, chopped

1 clove garlic, minced

½ teaspoon dried basil

Two 15-ounce cans peeled Italian plum tomatoes, undrained

½ teaspoon black pepper, or to taste

½ teaspoon cayenne pepper, or to taste

One 16-ounce can creamed corn

In a medium saucepan, bring the water, oil, and salt to a boil over high heat. Stir in the brown rice. Reduce the heat to low and simmer, covered, for about 50 minutes, until the rice is tender. Drain the rice if necessary, and set aside.

Spray a large saucepan with nonstick cooking spray and heat over medium heat. Add the turkey, onion, and garlic and cook for about 5 minutes, until the turkey loses its pink color, stirring often to break up the turkey.

Drain off any excess liquid, then stir in the basil, tomatoes with their juice, black pepper, and cayenne pepper, stirring to break up the tomatoes. Reduce the heat to medium-low, cover, and simmer for 20 minutes, stirring occasionally.

Add the creamed corn and cooked brown rice and cook for about 5 minutes, until heated through.

NUTRITIONAL CONTENT PER SERVING: Calories: 269   Protein: 11 g
Carbohydrates: 40 g   Fat: 6 g   Saturated fat: 2 g   Cholesterol: 24 mg
Sodium: 380 mg   Fiber: 5 g   21 percent calories from fat

White Bean–Tomato Soup

Firefighter Mark Hetzel
Green Township Fire Department
Cincinnati, Ohio

Serves 8

Cabbage, potatoes, and a good amount of white beans make this an especially satisfying and filling soup.

¾ cup dried Great Northern beans, rinsed
6 cups water
1 tablespoon olive oil
1 cup chopped onion
¾ cup chopped carrots
1 cup chopped celery with leaves
1¾ cups beef broth, preferably homemade (page 112), or canned
    low-sodium broth
One 15-ounce can peeled Italian plum tomatoes, undrained
2 cups shredded cabbage
1 baking potato, peeled and diced
¼ cup chopped fresh parsley
1 teaspoon dried basil
½ teaspoon dried thyme
1 teaspoon salt
¼ teaspoon black pepper
2 zucchini, chopped
1 cup water (optional)

Put the Great Northern beans in a large soup pot and add enough cold water to cover by 2 inches. Bring to a boil over high heat and cook for 2 minutes. Remove from the heat, cover, and let stand for 1 hour. Or, in a medium bowl, soak the beans in 2 quarts of water at room temperature overnight. Drain the beans completely and rinse the pot.

Return the beans to the soup pot and add 6 cups of water. Bring the beans to a boil, reduce the heat to low, and simmer, covered, for about 1½ hours, until the beans are tender. Cooking time will depend on the beans' freshness.

Transfer a third to a half of the beans with their cooking liquid to an electric blender or food processor. Blend until smooth. Transfer to a medium bowl. Repeat the process with the remaining beans and cooking liquid in as many batches as necessary and add to the pureed beans. Set the pureed beans aside.

Wash the soup pot and pour in the oil. Heat over medium heat. Add the onion, carrots, and celery. Cover and cook for about 5 minutes, until the vegetables soften. Stir in the beef broth, tomatoes with their juice, cabbage, potato, parsley, basil, thyme, salt, and pepper. Bring the mixture to a boil, stirring with a wooden spoon to break up the tomatoes. Reduce the heat to low, cover, and simmer for 15 minutes. Add the zucchini, cover again, and cook for about 10 minutes, until all the vegetables are tender. If the soup is too thick, add another cup of water. Serve hot.

NUTRITIONAL CONTENT PER SERVING: **Calories: 140   Protein: 7 g**
Carbohydrates: 25 g   Fat: 2 g   Saturated fat: 0 g   Cholesterol: 0 mg
Sodium: 545 mg   Fiber: 3 g   14 percent calories from fat

Hungry Firefighters Chili

Firefighter Paul Nethercott
Emerald Society Pipe and Drum
Westchester Fire Department
Westchester, New York

Serves 8

Just about every big-city fire department has a bagpipe and drum corps that marches proudly in parades and honors our fallen brothers and sisters at funerals. Westchester's Emerald Society Pipe and Drum is such a corps, and I am sure this feisty chili keeps them well fed.

1½ pounds ground turkey
1 large onion, chopped
1 green bell pepper, seeded and chopped
2 fresh hot green peppers (such as jalapeño), seeded and chopped, or one
     14-ounce can chopped green chiles, drained
4 cloves garlic, minced
Two 15-ounce cans red kidney beans, drained
Two 16-ounce cans chopped tomatoes, undrained
One 15-ounce can tomato sauce
1 teaspoon dried basil
3 tablespoons chili powder, or to taste
2 teaspoons crushed hot red pepper flakes, or to taste
3 tablespoons hot red pepper sauce
1 teaspoon black pepper

Combine the turkey, onion, green pepper, hot peppers, and garlic in a large saucepan over medium-high heat and cook for about 5 minutes, until the turkey is browned.

Drain off the excess liquid. Add the kidney beans, tomatoes with their juice, tomato sauce, basil, chili powder, red pepper flakes, red pepper sauce, and black pepper.

Stir, cover, and simmer for 20 minutes over low heat. Serve hot.

NUTRITIONAL CONTENT PER SERVING: **Calories: 225   Protein: 17 g
Carbohydrates: 26 g   Fat: 7 g   Saturated fat: 2 g   Cholesterol: 28 mg
Sodium: 615 mg   Fiber: 4 g   26 percent calories from fat**

Smokehouse Seafood Chowder

The day a probationary firefighter enters the smokehouse is the day he or she decides if firefighting is really the right career choice. The smokehouse is a brick and steel building where instructors seal doors and windows and then fill the interior with smoke by laying damp hay over fires burning in barrels. The firefighters-in-training must crawl through the smoke, following a hose line on the floor, without benefit of air masks. This is where the term "smoke eater" comes from, and the experience brings home the point that firefighting involves a lot more than riding around on a shiny red truck and wearing a fancy uniform at parades. I named this chowder after the smokehouse because of its unmistakable smoky flavor.

1 tablespoon canola or other vegetable oil
1 small chopped onion
1 large baking potato, peeled and cut into ½-inch cubes
1 cup dry white wine
2 springs fresh thyme or ¼ teaspoon dried thyme
1 tablespoon chopped fresh dill
3 cups skim milk
2 ripe tomatoes, seeded and chopped
6 ounces bay scallops
4 ounces smoked salmon, bluefish, or trout, coarsely chopped
12 ounces boneless halibut or cod, cut into 1-inch pieces
1 teaspoon prepared liquid smoke flavoring
¼ teaspoon salt
¼ teaspoon black pepper

In a large soup pot, heat the oil over medium heat. Add the onion, cover, and cook for about 5 minutes, until the onion softens. Add the potato, wine, thyme, and dill. Reduce the heat to low, cover, and simmer for about 20 minutes, until the potato is tender.

Using a potato masher or fork, coarsely mash the potato in the pot. Stir in the milk, tomatoes, scallops, smoked fish, fresh fish, and smoke flavoring. Cook for about 7 minutes, until the fish and scallops are firm but not rubbery. Season to taste with the salt and pepper and serve hot.

NUTRITIONAL CONTENT PER SERVING: **Calories: 198** **Protein: 18 g**
Carbohydrates: 17 g **Fat: 4 g** **Saturated fat: 1 g** **Cholesterol: 36 mg**
Sodium: 268 mg **Fiber: 1 g** **20 percent calories from fat**

Turkey and Black Bean Chili

Firefighter Robert Kelly   Serves 8
Ladder Company 160
New York City Fire Department
Queens, New York

I met Bob when we were both on temporary duty as fire inspectors in District Office 3 in midtown Manhattan. We worked out together several times, and I was duly impressed with his Fire Academy record of 37 pull-ups—which he holds to this day.

continued

1 pound ground turkey

1 onion, chopped

1 cup chopped celery

½ cup shredded carrot

1 fresh hot green chile pepper (such as jalapeño), seeded and minced, or
    ¼ cup drained canned chopped green chiles

2 cloves garlic, finely chopped

1½ tablespoons chili powder

1 teaspoon ground cumin

½ teaspoon salt

Two 28-ounce cans crushed tomatoes

Two 16-ounce cans black beans, drained and rinsed

In a large nonstick skillet, cook the ground turkey, onion, celery, carrot, chile pepper, and garlic over medium heat for about 6 minutes, until the turkey loses its pink color, stirring often to break up the turkey. Drain off any excess liquid and transfer the mixture to a large soup pot.

Add the chili powder, cumin, and salt and stir for 1 minute. Stir in the crushed tomatoes and black beans and bring to a simmer. Reduce the heat and simmer, uncovered, for about 30 minutes, stirring occasionally. Serve hot.

NUTRITIONAL CONTENT PER SERVING: **Calories: 317** **Protein: 21 g**
Carbohydrates: 31 g **Fat: 10 g** **Saturated fat: 2 g** **Cholesterol: 24 mg**
Sodium: 665 mg **Fiber: 14 g** **26 percent calories from fat**

Quebec Cabbage Soup

Firefighter Sylvie LaCombe
Volunteer Fire Department
Mount St. Hilaire, Quebec

Serves 4

Sylvie was the first firefighter from another country to send me a recipe for the book. She belongs to a small volunteer fire department in a town not too far from Montreal. I'm sure she and her fellow firefighters appreciate this warming all-vegetable soup during Canada's long winters.

1 cup shredded green cabbage
¼ cup finely chopped onion
¼ cup finely chopped carrot
1 tablespoon minced shallot or scallion
1 clove garlic, finely chopped
4 cups chicken broth, preferably homemade (page 110), or canned
    low-sodium broth
⅛ teaspoon salt
⅛ teaspoon black pepper
1 tablespoon chopped fresh parsley

Spray a medium saucepan with nonstick cooking spray. Add the cabbage, onion, carrot, shallot, and garlic. Cover and cook over medium-low heat for about 5 minutes, until the vegetables soften. Add the chicken broth, salt, and pepper. Bring to a simmer and cook, partially covered, for about 20 minutes, until the vegetables are very tender. Serve hot, garnished with parsley.

NUTRITIONAL CONTENT PER SERVING: Calories: 33   Protein: 3 g
Carbohydrates: 4 g   Fat: 1 g   Saturated fat: 0 g   Cholesterol: 0 mg
Sodium: 360 mg   Fiber: 1 g   21 percent calories from fat

Stick-to-Your-Ribs Stew

When I first introduced the idea of "healthy" meals to the firehouse, I met with resistant comments such as "I need food that will stick to my ribs!" Although the ribs have nothing to do with digestion, I understand that this means food that both is satisfying to eat and won't leave you hungry anytime soon. This stew meets these criteria and then some!

2 pounds skinless, boneless turkey thighs, cut into 1½-inch pieces
1½ cups water
1 cup beef broth, preferably homemade (page 112) or canned low-sodium broth
¼ cup chopped fresh parsley
1 teaspoon salt
¾ teaspoon dried basil
½ teaspoon dried rosemary
¼ teaspoon black pepper
6 carrots, cut into 1-inch pieces
1½ pounds small whole mushrooms, halved vertically if large
6 ounces white boiling onions, peeled
¾ cup wild rice, rinsed
¾ cup dry red wine
One 10-ounce package frozen peas, thawed

Preheat the oven to 375°F.

Spray a large skillet with nonstick cooking spray and heat over medium heat. Put enough turkey into the skillet to fill the pan without crowding. Cook for about 8 minutes, until it is browned on all sides. Remove the turkey from the skillet and repeat the process with the remainder in as many batches as necessary.

Transfer the browned turkey to a large Dutch oven. Stir in the water, beef broth, parsley, salt, basil, rosemary, and pepper. Cover and bake for 1 hour.

Add the carrots, mushrooms, onions, wild rice, and wine. Stir well, cover the Dutch oven, and bake for about 1 hour more, until the rice is tender. Stir in the peas, return the stew to the oven, and bake for 10 minutes more. Remove from the oven and let stand for 5 minutes. Skim any fat off the surface of the sauce. Serve immediately.

NUTRITIONAL CONTENT PER SERVING: Calories: 267   Protein: 24 g
Carbohydrates: 22 g   Fat: 6 g   Saturated fat: 2 g   Cholesterol: 61 mg
Sodium: 507 mg   Fiber: 5 g   20 percent calories from fat

Broccoli-Cauliflower Soup

This is a creamy soup without any cream. I use skim milk thickened with cornstarch to achieve the consistency and then depend on the pureed vegetables to do the rest. This soup is terrifically healthful because it is made from both broccoli and cauliflower, two cruciferous vegetables recognized as great sources of beta carotene, a guard against some forms of cancer.

1 tablespoon canola or other vegetable oil
1 medium onion, chopped
2 stalks celery, chopped
2 cups chicken broth, preferably homemade (page 110), or canned
      low-sodium broth
2 cups cauliflower florets
1½ cups broccoli florets
4 cups cold skim milk
2 tablespoons cornstarch
½ teaspoon dried thyme
½ teaspoon salt
¼ teaspoon black pepper

In a large soup pot, heat the oil over medium heat. Add the onion and celery, cover, and cook for about 5 minutes, until the onion softens. Add the broth and bring the mixture to a simmer. Add the cauliflower and broccoli, cover, reduce the heat to low, and simmer for about 10 minutes, until the vegetables are tender.

In a small bowl, whisk the milk, cornstarch, thyme, salt, and pepper until the mixture is smooth. Add the cornstarch mixture to the soup. Cook for about 3 minutes, stirring constantly, until the soup is slightly thickened and the mixture is just beginning to boil.

Remove from the heat. Transfer the soup in batches to a food processor or blender and puree. If necessary, return the pureed soup to the soup pot and simmer for 1 to 2 minutes to heat through. Serve hot.

NUTRITIONAL CONTENT PER SERVING: **Calories: 105   Protein: 9 g**
Carbohydrates: 13 g   Fat: 2 g   Saturated fat: 1 g   Cholesterol: 5 mg
Sodium: 232 mg   Fiber: 1 g   17 percent calories from fat

False-Alarm Vegetable Chili

I named this "false alarm" chili because it has no meat in it, as most chilies do. This is a delicious false alarm, although, quite frankly, many actual false alarms are malicious. They take us away from the firehouse when a true fire alarm may come in. If the company is not around to respond, another fire company is called in that may not be geographically nearby and thus will waste valuable, perhaps life-and-death, time getting to the site.

2 tablespoons olive oil

1 onion, chopped

1 green bell pepper, seeded and cut into ½-inch pieces

1 red bell pepper, seeded and cut into ½-inch pieces

1 carrot, chopped

1 fresh hot green chile pepper (such as jalapeño), seeded and finely chopped, or ¼ cup drained canned chopped green chiles

2 cloves garlic, finely chopped

7 cups water

1 pound dried lentils, rinsed

⅓ cup tomato paste

One 15-ounce can red kidney beans, drained and rinsed

One 15-ounce can pinto beans, drained and rinsed

One 28-ounce can stewed tomatoes

⅓ cup chili powder

4 teaspoons ground cumin

¼ teaspoon crushed hot red pepper flakes

¼ teaspoon salt
¼ teaspoon black pepper

In a large soup pot, heat the olive oil over medium heat. Add the onion, green and red peppers, carrot, chile pepper, and garlic. Cook for about 5 minutes, until the vegetables soften. Stir in the water, lentils, tomato paste, kidney beans, and pinto beans. Stir to blend, then add the stewed tomatoes, chili powder, cumin, and crushed red pepper flakes.

Bring to a boil. Reduce the heat to medium-low, cover, and simmer for 45 minutes, until the lentils are tender. If the chili starts to dry out, add hot water as needed. Season with salt and pepper and serve immediately.

NUTRITIONAL CONTENT PER SERVING: Calories: 390   Protein: 18 g
Carbohydrates: 68 g   Fat: 6 g   Saturated fat: 1 g   Cholesterol: 0 mg
Sodium: 289 mg   Fiber: 12 g   14 percent calories from fat

Garden Patch Stew

Firefighter Joseph Bruni
Master Station
St. Petersburg Fire Department
St. Petersburg, Florida

Serves 8

This low-fat meatless stew, which comes from a firefighter in Florida, is made with eggplant, which is a wonderful vegetable for providing body. Eggplant works best in stews and other dishes if it is salted and drained first. The salt pulls excess moisture from the eggplant so that it holds up during cooking. Be sure to rinse it very well after salting and draining it. The recipe also calls for grated lemon zest. Use only the yellow part of the peel—not the bitter white pith.

Two 1-pound eggplants, peeled and cut into 1-inch cubes
1 tablespoon olive oil
1 medium onion, sliced
2 cloves garlic, finely chopped
2 medium zucchini, sliced ½ inch thick
¼ cup chopped fresh parsley
2 tablespoon chopped fresh basil or 2 teaspoons dried basil
Grated zest of 1 lemon
1 cup plain nonfat yogurt
1 teaspoon Dijon mustard
1 teaspoon prepared horseradish
½ teaspoon honey
3 tomatoes, peeled, seeded, and chopped
Salt and pepper to taste

Put the eggplant in a colander and sprinkle liberally with salt. Let drain for about 15 minutes. Rinse well and drain.

In a large nonstick skillet, heat the oil over medium-high heat. Add the onion and garlic, cover, and cook for about 5 minutes, until the onion softens. Add the eggplant, zucchini, parsley, basil, and lemon zest. Reduce the heat to medium-low and simmer, covered, for about 20 minutes, until the eggplant is tender.

In a small bowl, mix the yogurt, mustard, horseradish, and honey. Cover and refrigerate.

Add the tomatoes to the stew and cook for about 5 minutes, until they soften. Serve the stew hot, topped with dollops of the yogurt dressing.

NUTRITIONAL CONTENT PER SERVING: **Calories: 100   Protein: 4 g**
Carbohydrates: 18 g   Fat: 3 g   Saturated fat: 0 g   Cholesterol: 1 mg
Sodium: 55 mg   Fiber: 6 g   21 percent calories from fat

Sweet Potato Soup

I use sweet potatoes whenever I can because they are one of the very best sources of complex carbohydrates and are high in cancer-fighting beta carotene. Cooked, they release a wonderful sugary flavor. Try this creamy soup to discover how good they are!

1 tablespoon canola or other vegetable oil
1 medium onion, chopped
5 cups chicken broth, preferably homemade (page 110), or canned
    low-sodium broth
2 large sweet potatoes, peeled and cut into 1-inch cubes
½ teaspoon grated nutmeg
¼ teaspoon salt
¼ teaspoon black pepper
1 cup low-fat milk

In a large soup pot, heat the oil over medium heat. Add the onion and cook for about 5 minutes, until softened. Stir in the broth, sweet potatoes, nutmeg, salt, and pepper. Cover and bring to a boil over high heat.

Reduce the heat to low and simmer, uncovered, for about 30 minutes, until the sweet potatoes are tender. Remove from the heat, transfer the solids and a little of the liquid to a blender or food processor, and puree. Transfer to a saucepan, add the milk, and reheat for about 10 minutes, until the soup is heated through but not boiling. Serve hot.

NUTRITIONAL CONTENT PER SERVING: **Calories: 285   Protein: 10 g
Carbohydrates: 53 g   Fat: 4 g   Saturated fat: 1 g   Cholesterol: 0 mg
Sodium: 549 mg   Fiber: 5 g   13 percent calories from fat**

El Diablo Sausage and Lentil Stew

Serves 8

The firefighters in my company dig into this for lunch. I make a tremendous, firehouse-size pot on chilly New York afternoons and leave it barely simmering on the back of the stove. By the end of the day tour, there is not a drop left. And we've all gotten a good dose of protein, carbohydrates, and fiber without a lot of fat.

1 tablespoon olive oil

8 ounces hot Italian turkey sausage, pierced with a fork

8 ounces sweet Italian turkey sausage, pierced with a fork

1 medium onion, chopped

2 cloves garlic, minced

6 cups chicken broth, preferably homemade (page 110), or canned
    low-sodium broth

1½ cups water

1 pound dried lentils, rinsed

One 28-ounce can low-sodium stewed tomatoes

½ teaspoon dried oregano

½ teaspoon dried tarragon

½ teaspoon black pepper

½ teaspoon sugar

¼ teaspoon hot red pepper sauce, or to taste

In a large soup pot, heat the oil over medium heat. Add the sausages and cook for about 8 minutes, until they are browned on all sides.

continued

Remove the sausages from the pot and drain off all but 1 tablespoon of fat. Slice the sausages ¼ inch thick and return them to the pot.

Add the onion and garlic and cook for about 3 minutes, stirring often, until the onion softens. Add the chicken broth, water, and lentils, stir, and bring to a boil.

Cover, reduce the heat to low, and simmer for about 30 minutes. Stir in the tomatoes, oregano, tarragon, black pepper, sugar, and hot sauce. Increase the heat to high and bring the stew to a boil, stirring often. Reduce the heat to low and simmer for about 20 minutes, until the lentils are tender. Serve immediately.

NUTRITIONAL CONTENT PER SERVING: Calories: 475   Protein: 36 g
Carbohydrates: 53 g   Fat: 14 g   Saturated fat: 5 g   Cholesterol: 35 mg
Sodium: 266 mg   Fiber: 11 g   26 percent calories from fat

Bread Soup

Serves 6

Bread soup may sound odd to the uninitiated, but once you try it, you'll be a convert. The secret to success is to buy the best bread you can. If you have an Italian market or bakery in the neighborhood, make a special trip. The zesty cabbage soup is ladled over garlic-flavored bread, which softens as you eat the soup and mingles nicely with the flavors. The bread also makes this soup more filling than it would otherwise be.

4 cups water
1 teaspoon salt
Two 16-ounce cans red kidney beans, drained and rinsed
1 tablespoon olive oil

3 ounces turkey bacon, chopped

1½ cups shredded cabbage

1 onion, finely chopped

1 stalk celery, finely chopped

1 fresh hot red chile pepper, seeded and finely chopped, or ¼ teaspoon
   crushed hot red pepper flakes

1 clove garlic, minced

1¼ pounds ripe plum tomatoes, seeded and coarsely chopped, or one
   28-ounce can peeled Italian plum tomatoes, drained and chopped

½ cup chopped fresh parsley

1 tablespoon dried basil

¼ teaspoon black pepper

6 slices crusty Italian bread, each cut to fit the bottom of a soup bowl

1 whole clove garlic, peeled

In a large soup pot, heat the water, salt, and beans over medium heat and bring to a simmer.

Meanwhile, in a large nonstick skillet, heat the oil over medium heat. Add the turkey bacon, cabbage, onion, celery, chile pepper, and minced garlic. Cook, covered, for about 5 minutes, until the vegetables soften. Transfer the mixture to the bean pot and then stir in the tomatoes, parsley, and basil. Simmer for about 30 minutes, until all the vegetables are very tender. Season with black pepper.

Toast the bread and rub each piece all over with the whole clove of garlic. Place a piece of toast in each bowl. Pour the soup over the bread and serve immediately.

NUTRITIONAL CONTENT PER SERVING: **Calories: 285   Protein: 13 g**
Carbohydrates: 46 g   Fat: 6 g   Saturated fat: 1 g   Cholesterol: 5 mg
Sodium: 1,203 mg   Fiber: 11 g   19 percent calories from fat

Spinach Siren Soup

Firefighter Richard Curiel

Serves 8

Ladder Company 130

New York City Fire Department

Queens, New York

Fresh spinach, which is a rich source of beta carotene, vitamin C, and iron, tends to cook down to practically nothing. In this soup it is added at the very end so that it keeps some of its shape and springy texture.

1 tablespoon olive oil

1 pound extra-lean ground sirloin

1 medium onion, chopped

1 clove garlic, finely chopped

One 8-ounce can tomato sauce

¼ teaspoon salt

¼ teaspoon black pepper

7 cups beef broth, preferably homemade (page 112), or canned low-sodium broth

1 cup corn kernels, fresh or frozen and defrosted

½ cup long-grain white rice

1 pound spinach, washed well, stems removed, and cut into ½-inch-wide strips

In a large saucepan, heat the oil over medium-high heat. Add the ground beef, onion, and garlic and cook for about 7 minutes, until the meat loses its pink color, stirring often to break up the beef. Stir in the tomato sauce, salt, and pepper.

Cover and cook over medium heat for 10 to 15 minutes, stirring occasionally. Stir in the broth, cover, and bring the soup to a boil. Add the corn and rice, cover again, and continue cooking for 15 to 20 minutes, until the rice is tender. Stir in the spinach, cover, and simmer gently for 5 minutes. Serve hot.

NUTRITIONAL CONTENT PER SERVING: **Calories: 385   Protein: 23 g Carbohydrates: 31 g   Fat: 6 g   Saturated fat: 2 g   Cholesterol: 52 mg Sodium: 552 mg   Fiber: 5 g   20 percent calories from fat**

Chunky Turkey Chili

Here is another turkey chili, one that I dreamed up as a way to use leftover turkey. Turkey is a wonderful meat to use in place of beef and pork because it is so comparatively low in fat.

2 tablespoons olive oil

2 large onions, chopped

2 medium green bell peppers, seeded and coarsely chopped

4 cloves garlic, chopped

Two 35-ounce cans plum tomatoes, undrained

One 15-ounce can tomato puree

¼ cup chili powder

4 teaspoons ground cumin

1 tablespoon hot red pepper flakes

½ teaspoon salt

1 tablespoon dried oregano

½ teaspoon ground cinnamon

½ teaspoon black pepper

⅛ teaspoon ground red pepper

4 cups cubed cooked skinless turkey meat

Two 19-ounce cans kidney beans, drained and rinsed

In a large soup pot, heat the oil over medium heat. Add the onions, green peppers, and garlic. Cover and cook for about 5 minutes, until the vegetables soften.

Add the tomatoes and their juice, tomato puree, chili powder, cumin, red pepper flakes, salt, oregano, cinnamon, black pepper, and ground red pepper. Break up the tomatoes with a spoon. Stir in the turkey and reduce the heat to low.

Simmer, uncovered, for about 2 hours, stirring occasionally, until the mixture has thickened. Add the kidney beans and simmer for about 10 minutes more, until the beans are heated through. Serve immediately.

NUTRITIONAL CONTENT PER SERVING: **Calories: 370   Protein: 35 g**
Carbohydrates: 33 g   Fat: 12 g   Saturated fat: 3 g   Cholesterol: 77 mg
Sodium: 936 mg   Fiber: 13 g   29 percent calories from fat

Chicken Broth

Often the butcher will sell you chicken parts very inexpensively if you explain that you are using them for stock. If you eat a lot of chicken, save the backs and wings when you cut up the chicken for other uses. Remember when making stock that the vegetables only need to be washed well and coarsely chopped. You do not have to peel the carrots, although you should take off most of the papery skin from the onion and garlic. Add as much or as little salt as you desire. If you prefer low- or no-sodium broth, make it that way. To freeze broth, chill it first and, after removing the surface fat, transfer it to a plastic container with a tight-fitting lid. You might want to freeze it in cup-size containers so that you only need take a cup or two from the freezer at any one time.

2 whole chickens, about 3 pounds each, rinsed and roughly chopped, or
    5 pounds chicken parts such as backs and wings
1 large onion, chopped
2 pounds carrots, chopped
2 bunches celery with leaves, sliced
4 cloves garlic, finely chopped
1 bunch fresh parsley, chopped
1 teaspoon salt (optional)
½ teaspoon black pepper

Put the chicken, onion, carrots, celery, garlic, and parsley in a stockpot and add enough cold water to cover the chicken and vegetables by 2 inches. Bring the mixture to a boil over high heat; skim off any foam that rises to the surface.

If you are using whole chickens, reduce the heat to medium-low and cook for about 1 hour, until the meat is tender. Remove the chickens from the soup, take the meat off the bones and reserve it, refrigerated, for another use. Return the carcasses to the pot and simmer the broth for 30 minutes longer. Season with salt and pepper if desired. Remove the broth from the heat; strain and discard all the solids.

If you are using chicken parts, simmer over very low heat, partially covered, for about 3 hours. Remove the chicken parts from the broth. Take the meat from the bones if possible (this may not be worth the effort with backs and wings). Reserve any chicken parts with meat and any removed meat, refrigerated, for another use, or discard them. Return any bones to the pot and let the broth simmer for 30 minutes more. Season with salt and pepper if desired. Remove the broth from the heat; strain and discard all the solids.

Let the broth cool slightly and then refrigerate it for at least 4 hours. Skim off any fat that solidifies on the surface. Use the broth within a day or so, or freeze it for up to 3 months.

NUTRITIONAL CONTENT PER SERVING: (1 serving = 1 cup)
Calories: 45   Protein: 8 g   Carbohydrates: 0 g   Fat: 1 g   Saturated fat: 0 g
Cholesterol: 7 mg   Fiber: 0 g   25 percent calories from fat

Beef Broth

When buying bones for beef broth, either ask the butcher for bones, telling him you will be using them for stock and requesting those with more meat than fat, or buy inexpensive cuts of meat with bone at the supermarket. Remember when making stock that the vegetables only need to be washed well and coarsely chopped. You do not have to peel the carrots, although you should take off most of the papery skin from the onion and garlic. Add as much or as little salt as you desire. If you prefer low- or no-sodium broth, make it that way. To freeze broth, chill it first and, after removing the surface fat, transfer it to a plastic container with a tight-fitting lid. You might want to freeze it in cup-size containers so that you only need take a cup or two from the freezer at any one time.

5 pounds meaty beef bones
1 cup boiling water
1 large onion, diced
2 pounds carrots, chopped
2 bunches celery with leaves, sliced
4 cloves garlic, finely chopped
1 bunch fresh parsley, chopped
1 teaspoon salt (optional)
½ teaspoon black pepper

Preheat the oven to 400°F. Spread the beef bones in a baking pan and roast them for about 1 hour, until very brown. Turn them once or twice during roasting. Remove the bones from the pan and transfer them to a stockpot.

Drain the fat from the roasting pan, add 1 cup of boiling water to it, and scrape up any browned bits that stick to the bottom with a wooden spoon. Transfer this to the stockpot.

Add the onion, carrots, celery, garlic, and parsley to the pot and add enough cold water to cover the bones and vegetables by 2 inches. Bring the mixture to a boil over high heat and skim off any foam that rises to the surface. Simmer over very low heat, partially covered, for 5 hours. Season with salt and pepper if desired. Remove the broth from the heat; strain and discard all the solids.

Let the broth cool slightly and then refrigerate it for at least 4 hours. Skim off any fat that solidifies on the surface. Use the broth within a day or so, or freeze it for up to 3 months.

NUTRITIONAL CONTENT PER SERVING: **(1 serving = 1 cup)**

Calories: 15   Protein: 2 g   Carbohydrates: 22 g   Fat: 1 g   Saturated fat: 0 g

Cholesterol: 6 mg   Sodium: 5 g   Fiber: 0 g   55 percent calories from fat

Pasta
and
Rice

Spaghetti with Old-Fashioned Tomato Pasta Sauce

Serves 6

We eat huge portions of pasta at the firehouse, and there's not a firefighter I've ever met who didn't like spaghetti with red sauce. This is my basic recipe, with two variations for enhancing the sauce with the addition of ground meat or seafood.

2 teaspoons olive oil
1 onion, finely chopped
1 clove garlic, minced
Two 28-ounce cans tomatoes in thick puree
2 teaspoons dried basil
2 teaspoons dried oregano
¼ teaspoon crushed hot red pepper flakes
1 pound spaghetti

In a large saucepan, heat the oil over medium heat. Add the onion and garlic and cook for about 5 minutes, stirring often, until the onion is golden. Stir in the tomatoes and puree, basil, oregano, and red pepper flakes. Bring to a simmer over medium-high heat, breaking up the tomatoes with the side of a spoon.

Reduce the heat to low and cook, uncovered or partially covered, for about 1½ hours, stirring often, until the mixture thickens and reduces in volume to about 5 cups and the tomatoes have lost their harsh, acid taste.

eanwhile, bring a large pot of salted water to a boil. Add the spaghetti and cook to taste, following the package directions. Drain well and transfer to a warmed large serving bowl. Toss the spaghetti with the sauce and serve immediately.

NUTRITIONAL CONTENT PER SERVING: **Calories: 375   Protein: 13 g**

Carbohydrates: 75 g   Fat: 3 g   Saturated fat: 0 g   Cholesterol: 0 mg

Sodium: 616 mg   Fiber: 8 g   8 percent calories from fat

Meaty Tomato Sauce: In a large nonstick skillet, heat the oil over medium heat. Add the onion, garlic, and 1 pound of ground turkey or Italian turkey sausage (casings removed). Cook for about 6 minutes, stirring with a wooden spoon to break up the meat, until the turkey loses its pink color. Drain off any liquid, transfer to a large saucepan, and proceed with the basic recipe at the point where the tomatoes, puree, and herbs are added to the pan.

NUTRITIONAL CONTENT PER SERVING: **Calories: 481   Protein: 26 g**

Carbohydrates: 75 g   Fat: 9 g   Saturated fat: 2 g   Cholesterol: 46 mg

Sodium: 665 mg   Fiber: 7 g   17 percent calories from fat

Fisherman's Spaghetti Sauce: Make the sauce according to the basic recipe and simmer for about 1½ hours, until it thickens. Just before tossing the sauce with the cooked pasta, stir in 1 pound fish fillets cut into 1-inch chunks. (Use scrod, snapper, cod, or flounder, or if you wish, use shellfish, such as scallops or shelled, deveined shrimp, or a combination.) Cook for about 5 minutes, until the fish is firm and opaque. Toss with the pasta and serve immediately.

NUTRITIONAL CONTENT PER SERVING: **Calories: 420   Protein: 22 g**

Carbohydrates: 75 g   Fat: 4 g   Saturated fat: 1 g   Cholesterol: 17 mg

Sodium: 645 mg   Fiber: 7 g   8 percent calories from fat

Spaghetti with Turkey Meatballs

Serves 8

Who doesn't like spaghetti and meatballs? No one I have ever ridden alongside of on a firetruck! Using ground turkey instead of beef saves calories and fat, and cooking the meatballs in the oven rather than in a skillet of oil helps too. The milk and eggs moisten the turkey, and the bread crumbs bind the meatballs together.

½ cup bread crumbs
¼ cup skim milk
2 large egg whites, beaten
1 small onion, minced
1 clove garlic, minced
1 teaspoon dried basil
1 teaspoon dried oregano
½ teaspoon salt
¼ teaspoon black pepper
1½ pounds ground turkey
1 pound spaghetti
5 cups Old-Fashioned Tomato Pasta Sauce (page 116)

Preheat the oven to 350°F. Lightly spray a baking sheet with nonstick cooking spray.

In a medium bowl, soak the bread crumbs in the milk for 5 minutes. Stir in the egg whites, onion, garlic, basil, oregano, salt, and pepper. Add the ground turkey and mix well.

Shape the mixture into 24 meatballs and place them about 1 inch apart on the baking sheet. Bake for about 12 minutes and then gently turn the meatballs. Continue baking for about 12 minutes longer, until the meatballs are firm and lightly browned.

Meanwhile, bring a large pot of salted water to a boil. Add the pasta and cook to taste, following the package directions. Drain well and transfer to a warmed large serving bowl. While the pasta is cooking, heat the pasta sauce in a large saucepan over medium heat until it is hot. Stir the sauce as it heats, taking care that it does not burn on the bottom.

When the sauce is hot, add half to the warm pasta. Top with the meatballs and pour the remaining sauce over them. Serve immediately.

NUTRITIONAL CONTENT PER SERVING: Calories: 413   Protein: 25 g
Carbohydrates: 58 g   Fat: 9 g   Saturated fat: 2 g   Cholesterol: 52 mg
Sodium: 584 mg   Fiber: 5 g   20 percent calories from fat

Pac Man Pasta

Firefighter JoAnne Lester   Serves 6
Engine Company 49
Philadelphia Fire Department
Philadelphia, Pennsylvania

This recipe came to me from a Philadelphia firefighter. I have always found it interesting that Benjamin Franklin, who was responsible for so much during our country's early days, is the man who founded the first organized fire department in Philly. As top-notch big-city forces, the New York and Philadelphia fire departments share many of the same century-old traditions and reputations.

1 tablespoon olive oil
1 pound medium mushrooms, quartered
2 cloves garlic, crushed through a press
1½ pounds asparagus, trimmed and sliced diagonally ½ inch thick
¼ cup fresh lemon juice
¼ teaspoon salt
⅛ teaspoon black pepper
1 pound rotelle (twist) pasta
¼ cup minced red bell pepper (about ¼ medium pepper)
2 ounces Parmesan cheese, in a chunk

Bring a large pot of lightly salted water to a boil.

In a large nonstick skillet, heat the oil over medium heat. Add the mushrooms and garlic and cook, covered, for about 5 minutes, until the mushrooms soften and release their juices. Add the asparagus and cook, covered, for about

3 minutes, until the asparagus is crisp-tender. Uncover and cook over medium-high heat for about 3 minutes, until most of the juices have evaporated. Add the lemon juice, salt, and pepper. Remove from the heat, transfer to a serving bowl, and keep warm.

Meanwhile, add the pasta to the boiling water and cook for about 10 minutes, until al dente. Drain, reserving 1 cup of the cooking water.

Add the drained pasta and reserved cooking water to the asparagus mixture and toss well. Stir in the red bell pepper. With a vegetable peeler, shave curls of the cheese over the top of the pasta and vegetables and serve immediately.

NUTRITIONAL CONTENT PER SERVING: **Calories: 284   Protein: 12 g
Carbohydrates: 19 g   Fat: 5 g   Saturated fat: 1 g   Cholesterol: 1 mg
Sodium: 64 mg   Fiber: 4 g   16 percent calories from fat**

Linguine with White Clam Sauce

Serves 6

Linguine and white clam sauce is a traditional dish in New York's Italian restaurants. It's also a great favorite of home cooks because canned minced clams are inexpensive and easy to find. My version is lighter than most but just as satisfying.

1 pound linguine
1 tablespoon olive oil
1 pound fresh mushrooms, sliced
2 cloves garlic, minced
Four 6½-ounce cans minced clams, drained and rinsed
½ cup fresh chopped parsley
½ cup dry white wine
¼ teaspoon salt
¾ teaspoon black pepper

Bring a large pot of lightly salted water to a boil, add the linguine, and cook for about 9 minutes, until al dente. Drain well and set aside. Keep warm.

In a large nonstick skillet, heat the olive oil over medium heat. Add the mushrooms and garlic and cook for about 5 minutes, until the mushrooms soften. Stir in the drained clams, parsley, wine, salt, and pepper. Simmer, uncovered, for about 2 minutes, until the mixture is thoroughly heated.

Add the linguine to the skillet and cook for 1 minute. Transfer to a serving bowl and toss well. Serve immediately.

NUTRITIONAL CONTENT PER SERVING: **Calories: 427** **Protein: 27 g**
Carbohydrates: 64 g **Fat: 5 g** **Saturated fat: 1 g** **Cholesterol: 41 mg**
Sodium: 170 mg **Fiber: 3 g** **11 percent calories from fat**

Fettuccine Feta Alfresco

Firefighter Doug Wetmore   **Serves 6**
Engine Station 1
Westminster Fire Department
Westminster, California

Straight from a California firefighter comes this simple, fast, and incredibly good pasta dish that combines the flavor of olives with feta cheese. The cheese melts just to the point of softening when tossed with the hot pasta. I think this tastes exactly like a dish from a sunny climate should.

1 pound fettuccine
1 tablespoon olive oil
3 cloves garlic, crushed through a press
8 ripe plum tomatoes, seeded and diced
4 ounces feta cheese, crumbled
½ cup chopped fresh basil
½ cup chopped pitted black olives, preferably Mediterranean

Bring a large pot of lightly salted water to a boil, add the fettuccine, and cook for about 10 minutes, until al dente. Drain well and set aside.

continued

In a large saucepan, heat the olive oil over medium heat. Add the garlic and stir for about 1 minute, until it is lightly browned.

In a large serving bowl, toss the cooked pasta with the browned garlic, tomatoes, cheese, basil, and olives. Mix well and serve immediately.

NUTRITIONAL CONTENT PER SERVING: **Calories: 300   Protein: 10 g**
Carbohydrates: 48 g   Fat: 8 g   Saturated fat: 3 g   Cholesterol: 13 mg
Sodium: 337 mg   Fiber: 4 g   24 percent calories from fat

DiGiovanni's Bronx Broccoli and Pasta

Firefighter Gary Iorio   Serves 4
Ladder Company 39
New York City Fire Department
Bronx, New York

I worked with Gary on a night tour in the Bronx, and we talked about putting together low-fat recipes. He was enthusiastic about this book and developed this recipe especially for it. In the spirit of good fun, he named it to rib a guy in his company named DiGiovanni, who adds huge amounts of butter to everything. This recipe has no butter, of course—but to make it "DiGiovanni-style," add about five sticks!

1½ pounds skinless, boneless chicken breasts, rinsed
1 head fresh broccoli
1 tablespoon olive oil

6 cloves garlic, finely chopped

1½ cups chicken broth, preferably homemade (page 110), or canned
low-sodium broth

1½ teaspoons dried oregano

1½ teaspoons dried basil

½ teaspoon black pepper

1 pound tubular pasta, such as ziti

Bring a large pot of lightly salted water to a boil.

Cut the chicken into 1-inch pieces, trimming off any visible fat.

Cut the broccoli into florets. Slice the stems crosswise ½ inch thick and set aside.

In a large nonstick skillet, heat the olive oil over medium heat. Add the garlic and stir for 30 seconds. Add the chicken pieces and cook for about 5 minutes, until the chicken is lightly browned on all sides. Add the broccoli, broth, oregano, basil, and pepper and bring to a simmer.

Cover and cook for about 7 minutes, until the broccoli is just tender.

Meanwhile, add the pasta to the boiling water and cook for about 10 minutes, until al dente. Drain well.

Transfer the pasta to a large serving bowl, add the broccoli mixture, and toss. Serve immediately.

NUTRITIONAL CONTENT PER SERVING: **Calories: 666   Protein: 51 g
Carbohydrates: 92 g   Fat: 10 g   Saturated fat: 2 g   Cholesterol: 87 mg
Sodium: 220 mg   Fiber: 8 g   18 percent calories from fat**

Class A Alfredo

Firefighter Jennifer Perley

Serves 3

Madbury Volunteer Fire Department

Madbury, New Hampshire

Jennifer has aptly named this rich yet low-fat, low-calorie recipe. Class A refers to a firefighter's dress uniform, the clothes we don when we want to look our very best. I always appreciate getting recipes from women firefighters. The field was male-dominated for so long, and it's refreshing to get to know some of the women who have joined our ranks. Unfortunately, it was only after years of struggle and numerous discrimination lawsuits that women were permitted to join. At that time our job title was officially changed to "firefighter" from "fireman."

1½ cups low-fat cottage cheese
2 cloves garlic, halved
½ cup skim milk
2 tablespoons all-purpose flour
1 tablespoon fresh lemon juice
1 teaspoon dried basil
½ teaspoon dry mustard
½ teaspoon black pepper
¼ teaspoon salt
8 ounces rotelle (twist) pasta
1 medium tomato, seeded and chopped

Bring a large pot of lightly salted water to a boil.

In a blender or food processor, blend the cottage cheese, garlic, and milk for 2 to 3 minutes, until very smooth. Stop and scrape down the sides of the bowl as needed. Add the flour, lemon juice, basil, mustard, pepper, and salt and blend well.

Meanwhile, add the pasta to the boiling water and cook it for about 8 minutes, until al dente. Drain and transfer to a large serving bowl and keep warm.

Transfer the cottage cheese mixture to a saucepan and heat over medium-low heat for about 3 minutes, until it thickens slightly. Stir constantly and be careful not to let it come to a boil.

Pour the heated cheese sauce over the pasta and toss well. Garnish with the tomato and serve immediately.

NUTRITIONAL CONTENT PER SERVING: **Calories: 196   Protein: 13 g**
Carbohydrates: 34 g   Fat: 1 g   Saturated fat: 0 g   Cholesterol: 3 mg
Sodium: 109 mg   Fiber: 2 g   4 percent calories from fat

Mama Minutoli's Macaroni Pie

Firefighter Louis Minutoli
Ladder Company 129
New York City Fire Department
Flushing, New York

Serves 4

I truly admire Louie's dedication to firefighting. Not only is he a full-time New York City firefighter but he is a commissioner of the West Hempstead Volunteer Fire Department on Long Island. This is one of his favorite quick firehouse meals: a macaroni pie held together with egg whites (which have no cholesterol) and flavored with tomatoes, cheese, parsley, and other good things.

8 ounces thin spaghetti
4 large egg whites
2 plum tomatoes, seeded and finely chopped
¼ cup grated Parmesan cheese
¼ cup chopped fresh parsley
¼ teaspoon salt
¼ teaspoon white pepper
1 clove garlic, minced
1 tablespoon chopped fresh basil

Bring a large pot of lightly salted water to a boil. Add the spaghetti and cook it for about 10 minutes, until al dente. Drain well.

Transfer to a medium bowl. Add the egg whites, tomatoes, cheese, parsley, salt, pepper, garlic, and basil and mix well. Spray a medium nonstick skillet with nonstick cooking spray and heat over medium heat.

Pour in the egg mixture and cook for about 3 minutes, until golden brown on the underside. Place a large plate on top of the skillet, hold it firmly with one hand, and invert the skillet with the other hand, so that the "pie" ends up on the plate, browned side up. Carefully slide the pie back into the skillet and cook for another 3 minutes, until the other side is browned. Serve the pie hot, cold, or at room temperature.

NUTRITIONAL CONTENT PER SERVING: **Calories: 307** **Protein: 13 g**
Carbohydrates: 43 g **Fat: 9 g** **Saturated fat: 3 g** **Cholesterol: 111 mg**
Sodium: 286 mg **Fiber: 3 g** **26 percent calories from fat**

Vegetarian Lasagna

Sylvia Vaher
Exercise Physiologist
Corporate Healthcare
St. Vincent's Hospital
New York, New York

Serves 12

Sylvia and I have worked together at several Corporate Wellness workshops, and believe me, she really knows her stuff when it comes to fitness and proper diet. Although she is not a firefighter, I am including her meatless lasagna. It's a terrific recipe that she recommends to her fitness clients and her friendly neighborhood firefighters.

9 lasagna noodles
1 tablespoon olive oil
8 ounces medium mushrooms, sliced
1 cup chopped onions (about 2 onions)
1 cup sliced celery (about 2 stalks)
1 cup thinly sliced carrots (about 1½ carrots)
2 cloves garlic, finely chopped
One 28-ounce can crushed tomatoes
One 6-ounce can tomato paste
1 teaspoon dried basil
½ teaspoon dried oregano
¾ teaspoon black pepper, divided
One 15-ounce container nonfat ricotta cheese
One 10-ounce package frozen chopped spinach, thawed and squeezed dry
1 large egg, beaten, or ¼ cup liquid egg substitute

1 clove garlic, crushed through a press

½ teaspoon salt

4 cups (about 1 pound) shredded part-skim mozzarella cheese, divided

¼ cup grated Parmesan cheese, divided

Preheat the oven to 350°F.

Bring a large pot of lightly salted water to a boil, add the lasagna noodles, and cook for about 10 minutes, until barely tender. Drain well, rinse under cold water, separate each noodle from the others to prevent sticking, and set aside.

In a large nonstick skillet, heat the olive oil over medium heat. Add the mushrooms, onions, celery, carrots, and chopped garlic. Cover and cook for about 5 minutes, until the vegetables soften. Stir in the crushed tomatoes, tomato paste, basil, oregano, and ¼ teaspoon of the black pepper. Simmer for 30 minutes.

Meanwhile, in a medium bowl, combine the ricotta cheese, spinach, egg, crushed garlic, salt, and remaining ½ teaspoon black pepper. Mix well.

In a lightly oiled 13-by-9-inch pan, lay 3 cooked lasagna noodles side by side. Top them with half of the ricotta mixture and a third of the tomato sauce. Cover with 3 more noodles, spread with the remaining ricotta mix, and slightly less than half of the remaining sauce. Sprinkle with half of the mozzarella and 2 tablespoons of the Parmesan cheese. Cover with the last 3 noodles, spread with the remaining tomato sauce, and sprinkle with the remaining mozzarella and Parmesan cheeses.

Transfer the pan to the oven and bake for about 30 minutes, until the lasagna bubbles throughout. Let stand for 10 minutes before serving.

NUTRITIONAL CONTENT PER SERVING: **Calories: 353   Protein: 25 g**
Carbohydrates: 41 g   Fat: 11 g   Saturated fat: 5 g   Cholesterol: 44 mg
Sodium: 596 mg   Fiber: 5 g   27 percent calories from fat

Shrimp Stuffed Shells

Stuffed shells are a favorite in the firehouse. They are filling enough for the hungriest firefighter yet not very high in fat or calories. Of course, stuffing them requires some patience, and I have to admit that most of my fellow firefighters prefer eating them to stuffing them. These are high in protein and low in fat.

18 jumbo macaroni shells
¼ cup all-purpose flour
½ cup skim milk
1¼ cups chicken broth, preferably homemade (page 110), or canned
    low-sodium broth
1 tablespoon tomato paste
1 teaspoon butter
1 pound uncooked medium shrimp, peeled and deveined
1 clove garlic, crushed through a press
2 cups (16 ounces) low-fat cottage cheese
2 large egg whites
2 tablespoons grated Parmesan cheese
2 tablespoons chopped fresh parsley
1 tablespoon minced fresh chives or 1 teaspoon dried chives
⅛ teaspoon black pepper
Chopped fresh basil or additional chopped fresh parsley

Preheat the oven to 350°F.

Bring a large pot of lightly salted water to a boil, add the macaroni shells, and cook for about 8 minutes, until the shells are barely tender. Drain, rinse under cold water, drain again, and set aside.

In a small saucepan, whisk together the flour and milk until smooth. Whisk in the broth and tomato paste. Bring to a boil over medium heat, whisking often. Reduce the heat to low, then simmer for about 2 minutes, until thickened. Set the sauce aside.

Spray a large nonstick skillet with nonstick cooking spray. Add the butter and melt it over high heat. Add the shrimp and cook for about 1 minute, stirring often. Reduce the heat to medium, add the garlic, and cook for 1 minute more, until the shrimp are firm and pink.

Transfer the shrimp and garlic to a work surface and chop coarsely. Put them in a bowl and stir in the cottage cheese, egg whites, Parmesan cheese, parsley, chives, and pepper.

Using a dessert spoon, stuff each pasta shell with the shrimp mixture. Pour half of the reserved white sauce into a lightly oiled 9-by-13-inch baking dish and arrange the stuffed shells in the pan. Cover the pan with foil and bake for 30 minutes, or until the sauce is bubbling throughout.

Reheat the remaining sauce over medium-low heat and pour over the shells just before serving. Sprinkle with the basil or parsley and serve immediately.

NUTRITIONAL CONTENT PER SERVING: (**1 serving = 2 shells**)
Calories: 250   Protein: 34 g   Carbohydrates: 19 g   Fat: 3 g   Saturated fat: 1 g
Cholesterol: 122 mg   Sodium: 406 mg   Fiber: 1 g   13 percent calories from fat

Enzo's Bean and Rice Delight

Firefighter Steven Fernandes   Serves 8
Engine Company 3
Linden Fire Department
Linden, New Jersey

There is a universal brotherhood among firefighters and I seem to run into firefighters wherever I travel. While vacationing with friends at Club Med in Huatulco, Mexico, I met Steve, the fitness instructor. After discussing various training regimens, Steve used an expression only a firefighter would know, and we realized we were both firefighters and became friends. This rice dish is made with brown rice, which needs longer cooking than white rice but has more nutrients because the vitamin-packed outer husk is not removed. The combination of rice and beans is classic in Mexico and other Latin countries and provides a complete protein allowance without the need for meat or fish.

2 pounds dried black beans, rinsed, or two 16-ounce cans black beans,
    drained and rinsed
3 tablespoons olive oil, divided
½ teaspoon salt
4 cups brown rice
1 medium onion, finely chopped
1 medium green bell pepper, seeded and chopped
1 medium red bell pepper, seeded and chopped
2 medium stalks celery, thinly sliced
1 medium carrot, thinly sliced
4 cloves garlic, finely chopped

½ teaspoon dried thyme

¼ cup cider vinegar

¼ teaspoon crushed hot red pepper flakes, or to taste

If you are using dried black beans, put them in a medium saucepan and add enough cold water to cover by 2 inches. Bring to a boil over high heat and cook for 2 minutes. Remove from the heat, cover, and let stand for 1 hour. Or, in a medium bowl, soak the beans overnight in 2 quarts of water at room temperature. Drain completely. Put the beans in a saucepan and cover with fresh water. Bring to a simmer over high heat, reduce to the heat to medium-low, and simmer, uncovered, for about 40 minutes, until the beans are tender. The cooking time will depend on the beans' freshness.

In another medium saucepan, bring 4½ cups water, 1 tablespoon of the oil, and the salt to a boil over high heat. Stir in the brown rice. Reduce the heat to low and simmer, covered, for about 50 minutes, until the rice is tender. Drain the rice if necessary, and set aside.

In a large soup pot, heat the remaining 2 tablespoons of oil over medium heat. Add the onion, bell peppers, celery, carrot, garlic, and thyme. Cook for about 10 minutes, stirring occasionally, until the vegetables are tender. Stir in the cooked or canned beans, rice, vinegar, and red pepper flakes. Continue to cook for about 5 minutes, stirring occasionally, until the dish is heated through. Serve hot.

NUTRITIONAL CONTENT PER SERVING: **Calories: 227   Protein: 9 g Carbohydrates: 40 g   Fat: 4 g   Saturated fat: 1 g   Cholesterol: 0 mg Sodium: 16 mg   Fiber 9 g   15 percent calories from fat**

Salsa Beans and Rice

Captain John Kostynick
Division 13
New York City Fire Department
New York, New York

Serves 10

Here's another easy way to serve the winning combination of beans and rice. This dish, too, relies on brown rice for lots of nutrients.

1 tablespoon olive oil, divided
½ teaspoon salt
2 cups brown rice
1 large onion, diced
2 stalks celery, diced
2 cloves garlic, finely chopped
3½ cups tomato sauce
One 16-ounce can red kidney beans, drained and rinsed
One 16-ounce can small white beans, drained and rinsed
One 16-ounce can black beans, drained and rinsed
½ cup prepared salsa
1 teaspoon dried oregano
⅛ teaspoon cayenne pepper
3 tablespoons chopped fresh cilantro (coriander)

In a medium saucepan, bring 4½ cups water, 1 tablespoon of the oil, and the salt to a boil over high heat. Stir in the brown rice. Reduce the heat to low and simmer, covered, for about 50 minutes, until the rice is tender. Drain the rice if necessary, and set aside.

In another medium saucepan, heat the remaining 1 tablespoon of oil over medium heat. Add the onion, celery, and garlic. Cover and cook for about 5 minutes, until the vegetables soften. Stir in the tomato sauce and cook for 5 minutes. Add the drained beans, salsa, oregano, and cayenne pepper. Bring to a simmer and cook over low heat for about 10 minutes. Stir in the cooked rice and cilantro and cook for about 3 minutes, until the dish is heated through. Serve hot.

NUTRITIONAL CONTENT PER SERVING: **Calories: 349   Protein: 15 g Carbohydrates: 68 g   Fat: 3 g   Saturated fat: 1 g   Cholesterol: 0 mg Sodium: 613 mg   Fiber: 12 g   7 percent calories from fat**

Stevie's Portuguese Rice

Firefighter Steven Fernandes

Engine Company 3

Linden Fire Department

Linden, New Jersey

Serves 8

This is one of those dishes that is so easy to make, you will do so over and over again. It's very low in fat and fairly high in complex carbohydrates—a great combination!

2 teaspoons olive oil

¼ teaspoon salt

1¼ cups brown rice

2 pounds lean ground turkey

1 medium onion, chopped

2 cloves garlic, finely chopped

Two 28-ounce cans peeled tomatoes, chopped, with juice

One 16-ounce can tomato sauce

1 teaspoon hot red pepper sauce, or to taste

½ teaspoon dried oregano

½ teaspoon black pepper

In a medium saucepan, bring 2¾ cups water, the oil, and salt to a boil over high heat. Add the brown rice, reduce the heat to low, and simmer, covered, for about 50 minutes, until the rice is tender. Drain the rice if necessary, and set aside.

Meanwhile, in a large nonstick skillet, cook the ground turkey, chopped onion, and garlic over medium heat for about 7 minutes, stirring occasionally, until the turkey loses its pink color. Stir in the tomatoes and their juice, tomato sauce, hot pepper sauce, oregano, and black pepper.

Bring to a simmer, reduce the heat to low, and cook, uncovered, for about 45 minutes. Stir in the cooked brown rice, simmer an additional 5 minutes, and serve immediately.

NUTRITIONAL CONTENT PER SERVING: **Calories: 225   Protein: 25 g**
Carbohydrates: 28 g   Fat: 2 g   Saturated fat: 1 g   Cholesterol: 58 mg
Sodium: 708 mg   Fiber: 4 g   8 percent calories from fat

Fish and Seafood

Crispy Spicy Catfish

Serves 4

It's more traditional to fry catfish in a pool of melted lard or oil, but I prefer oven-baking it with very little added fat and lots of flavor provided by hot sauce and seasonings. Cornmeal gives the fish a nice crispy crust. Most fish markets and supermarkets carry farm-raised catfish, a tender and tasty, versatile white-fleshed fish. You can substitute any white-fleshed fish, such as halibut or sole, but I urge you to try catfish if you can find it.

½ cup skim milk
1 teaspoon hot red pepper sauce
¾ cup yellow cornmeal
1 tablespoon Old Bay or Cajun seasoning
¼ teaspoon salt (optional)
1½ pounds catfish fillets
Lemon wedges

Preheat the oven to 400°F. Spray a baking sheet with nonstick cooking spray.

In a shallow bowl, combine the milk and hot pepper sauce. On a plate, combine the cornmeal and seasoning. (If using a salt-free seasoning, add the salt if you wish.) Dip each catfish fillet in the milk and then coat both sides with the cornmeal mixture. Transfer to the baking sheet.

Bake for 10 minutes, then turn each fillet with a spatula and bake for 10 minutes more, until the fish is opaque in the center when flaked with a fork. Garnish with lemon wedges and serve immediately.

NUTRITIONAL CONTENT PER SERVING: Calories: 195   Protein: 20 g
Carbohydrates: 20 g   Fat: 4 g   Saturated fat: 1 g   Cholesterol: 60 mg
Sodium: 77 mg   Fiber: 3 g   18 percent calories from fat

Fish for Sale

One evening a probie who was detailed to our firehouse offered to cook dinner. He explained that he had shopped during his off tour and had bought a sailfish. We assumed he was cooking swordfish, a luxury we all enjoyed, and so we happily agreed to the deal. No one was permitted in the kitchen as he worked, but as we went about our other duties checking tools and equipment, an aroma wafted out of the kitchen that was unfamiliar to everyone. The aroma soon turned into a genuine odor, and we anticipated our evening meal with waning enthusiasm.

"Chow's on," called the probie through the loudspeaker. We crept into the kitchen and sat down at the table, where a fish unlike any we had seen was lying on a bed of rice. The odor now resembled a bad low tide, and we glanced at each other nervously. But known across the land as "the bravest," we bravely flaked a little meat from the fish. We gagged. "What kind of fish is this?" we demanded. The probie, a city kid who had never left the five boroughs, proudly explained it was a fish he had gotten "real cheap" in his neighborhood: a sale fish!

We all had a great laugh and ordered out for pizza. The probie was demoted to peeling potatoes for a while and naturally became the brunt of endless fish jokes.

Poached Salmon with Sun-Dried Tomato Sauce

Firefighter Paul "Stache" Schulte
West Babylon Fire Department
West Babylon, New York

Serves 2

Firefighters do not normally have the time, money, or, quite frankly, inclination to prepare expensive "gourmet" dinners. The job demands that the meals we prepare at the firehouse be simple and use only a few ingredients or inexpensive, easy-to-find ones. But every once in a while, an exception to the rule is made, as it was for this salmon dish Paul gave me. I found I could put it together fairly inexpensively for one or two guys who were hankering for something special—even if it was served on the mismatched china and eaten with the bent flatware we are used to in the firehouse kitchen.

1 tablespoon olive oil
4 shallots, thinly sliced
2 cups chicken broth, preferably homemade (page 110), or canned
    low-sodium broth
1 cup white wine
12 whole black peppercorns
½ lemon, sliced
2 bay leaves
Two 6-ounce salmon fillets
6 oil-packed sun-dried tomatoes, rinsed and thinly sliced
2 tablespoons chopped fresh dill
⅛ teaspoon salt
⅛ teaspoon black pepper

In a small saucepan, heat the oil over low heat. Add the shallots and cook for about 2 minutes, stirring often, until they are translucent. Set aside.

In a large skillet, bring the broth, wine, peppercorns, lemon slices, and bay leaves to a simmer over low heat. Add the salmon, cover, and simmer for 8 to 10 minutes, just until the thickest part of the salmon is opaque when flaked with the tip of a knife. With a slotted spatula, transfer the salmon to dinner plates, and cover with foil to keep warm. Strain the cooking liquid and reserve ½ cup.

Stir the ½ cup of cooking liquid into the saucepan containing the shallots and add the sun-dried tomatoes, dill, salt, and pepper. Bring to a boil over medium heat. Reduce the heat to low and simmer for about 2 minutes. Pour the hot sauce over the salmon fillets and serve immediately.

NUTRITIONAL CONTENT PER SERVING: **Calories: 408   Protein: 46 g   Carbohydrates: 6 g   Fat: 21 g   Saturated fat: 3 g   Cholesterol: 125 mg   Sodium: 163 mg   Fiber 1 g   48 percent calories from fat**

Bob and Bob's Microwave Fish and Vegetables

Firefighters Bob Turk and Bob Sturm
Engine Company 72
Westlake Fire Department
Westlake, Ohio

Serves 4

Two Ohio firefighters named Bob submitted this fast and easy fish recipe, which has become something of a staple in our firehouse here in New York. Fillet of sole or flounder is nearly always available, and its mild flavor appeals to people who are not crazy about the taste of fish. Using the microwave makes preparation quick. The microwave is one of the best places to cook fish and vegetables—they come out nice and moist and rarely overcooked. Plus, you hardly have to add any fat.

2 7-ounce flounder or sole fillets
4 lemon slices
1 small red onion, thinly sliced
1 cup thinly sliced cauliflower florets
1 cup thinly sliced broccoli florets
1 zucchini, sliced ½ inch thick
1 large red bell pepper, seeded and sliced ½ inch thick
1 tomato, sliced ½ inch thick
1 tablespoon extra virgin olive oil
¼ teaspoon salt
⅛ teaspoon black pepper
2 tablespoons chopped fresh basil or parsley

Spray an 11-by-7-inch microwave-safe baking dish with nonstick cooking spray. Roll up each fish fillet into a thick cylinder and place in the dish, seam side down. Place 2 lemon slices on top of each rolled fillet.

Arrange the onion, cauliflower, broccoli, zucchini, and red pepper on top of the fish and top with tomato slices. Drizzle with olive oil. Cover with microwave-safe plastic wrap, folding back a corner to vent.

Microwave on high (100 percent) power for 7 to 10 minutes, until the fish is opaque when flaked with the tip of a knife. Season with salt and pepper and sprinkle with the basil or parsley. Cut each fillet in half crosswise and serve.

NUTRITIONAL CONTENT PER SERVING: **Calories: 188   Protein: 32 g**
Carbohydrates: 11 g   Fat: 2 g   Saturated fat: 1 g   Cholesterol: 73 mg
Sodium: 156 mg   Fiber: 4 g   11 percent calories from fat

Tuna Pasta Massella

Firefighter Robert Massella

Ladder Company 129

New York City Fire Department

Flushing, New York

Serves 6

When Bob's on duty, the clang of bodybuilding equipment can nearly always be heard from the basement of the firehouse. He is a serious bodybuilder who cares about protein-rich foods. He came up with this easy tuna supper that is high not only in protein but in valuable complex carbohydrates.

1 tablespoon olive oil

3 cloves garlic, sliced

Two 28-ounce cans stewed tomatoes

1 tablespoon dried oregano

1 tablespoon dried basil

½ teaspoon crushed hot red pepper flakes

1 pound linguine

Two 6⅛-ounce cans water-packed solid white tuna, drained

2 tablespoons chopped fresh parsley

In a large nonstick skillet, heat the oil over medium heat. Add the garlic and cook for about 1 minute, stirring often, until it is barely golden.

Add the tomatoes, oregano, basil, and red pepper flakes. Bring to a simmer, reduce the heat to low, and cook for about 20 minutes, until slightly thickened.

Meanwhile, bring a large pot of lightly salted water to a boil, add the linguine, and cook for about 9 minutes, until the pasta is just tender. Drain well and transfer to a heated serving bowl.

Stir the tuna into the tomato sauce and cook just to heat through. Pour the sauce over the pasta and sprinkle with the parsley. Toss well and serve immediately.

NUTRITIONAL CONTENT PER SERVING: **Calories: 468   Protein: 24 g
Carbohydrates: 76 g   Fat: 6 g   Saturated fat: 1 g   Cholesterol: 10 mg
Sodium: 873 mg   Fiber: 8 g   12 percent calories from fat**

Irish Baked Clams

Firefighter Thomas Collins
Ladder Company 129
New York City Fire Department
Flushing, New York

Makes 12 baked clams

Tom is a veteran who transferred to Ladder Company 129 after a long career in a notoriously busy firehouse, Ladder Company 14 in Harlem. While he worked there, he saved a woman's life by rescuing her from the top floor of an old brownstone, and for his valor he was awarded the coveted Hispanic Medal. Tom's appetite is as legendary as his bravery, and he particularly likes seafood. My appetite seems to match his, and we frequently indulge in these clams as an appetizer before an all-seafood dinner. You could also make them for dinner.

12 cherrystone clams, scrubbed well
¾ cup fresh whole wheat bread crumbs (about 1½ slices bread)
1 tablespoon minced green bell pepper
1 tablespoon minced onion
1 tablespoon minced celery
¼ teaspoon Worcestershire sauce
2 drops hot red pepper sauce
¼ cup grated Parmesan cheese
Paprika
2 teaspoons olive oil

Preheat the oven to 400°F.

If you haven't asked the fishmonger to do it for you, shuck the clams, reserving the juice and shells.

In a medium bowl, combine the bread crumbs, reserved clam juice, green pepper, onion, celery, Worcestershire sauce, and hot red pepper sauce. Put each shucked clam in a reserved shell and top with the crumb mixture.

Arrange the stuffed clams in a baking dish. If the clams rock, put crumpled foil in the dish and nestle the clams in the foil to secure them. Sprinkle each clam with 1 teaspoon of cheese and top with enough paprika to garnish. Drizzle each clam with oil.

Bake for 10 to 15 minutes, until the crumbs turn golden brown. Serve hot.

NUTRITIONAL CONTENT PER SERVING: (1 serving = 1 clam)

Calories: 58 Protein: 6 g Carbohydrates: 2 g Fat: 3 g Saturated fat: 0 g
Cholesterol: 16 mg Sodium: 129 mg Fiber: 0 g 39 percent calories from fat

Shrimp and Sausage Jambalaya

Firefighter Paul Jackson
Engine Company 20
Washington, D.C., Fire Department
Washington, D.C.

Serves 12

In this tomato-based one-dish meal, shrimp and turkey sausage go a long way. No one will believe this is low in fat and fairly low in calories. All it needs to make a complete meal is a green salad.

1 tablespoon olive oil
1 pound turkey kielbasa, sliced ½ inch thick
1 small green bell pepper, seeded and chopped
1 cup chopped celery
2 cloves garlic, minced
Two 16-ounce cans whole tomatoes, undrained
2 cups chicken broth, preferably homemade (page 110), or canned
    low-sodium broth
1 cup chopped scallions
¾ cup chopped fresh parsley
1 tablespoon Creole or Cajun seasoning
1 tablespoon dried oregano
1½ teaspoons dried thyme
2 bay leaves
¼ teaspoon ground red pepper
¼ teaspoon black pepper
2 cups long-grain white rice, rinsed well
3 pounds medium shrimp, peeled and deveined

In a large Dutch oven, heat the oil over medium heat. Add the kielbasa and cook for about 5 minutes, turning occasionally, until the sausage is browned. With a slotted spoon, transfer the sausage to a plate and set aside.

Add the green pepper, celery, and garlic to the Dutch oven and cook for about 5 minutes, stirring often, until the vegetables soften. Add the tomatoes with their juice, the chicken broth, scallions, parsley, seasoning, oregano, thyme, bay leaves, ground red pepper, and black pepper. Bring to a simmer and stir to break up the tomatoes. Stir in the rice and kielbasa and return to a simmer.

Reduce the heat to low, cover, and cook for 20 to 25 minutes, until the rice is just tender. Stir in the shrimp, cover, and cook for about 3 minutes more, until the shrimp turn pink. Let stand, covered, for 5 minutes before serving.

NUTRITIONAL CONTENT PER SERVING: **Calories: 362   Protein: 32 g
Carbohydrates: 32 g   Fat: 11 g   Saturated fat: 8 g   Cholesterol: 188 mg
Sodium: 798 mg   Fiber: 2 g   28 percent calories from fat**

Most Muscular Perch

Robin and Ranier Hartmann   Serves 4
Counselors, Muscle and Fitness Camp
Los Angeles, California

This is a recipe I got from two of the counselors I met at a fitness camp in California. Not only did I learn good bodybuilding techniques at camp but I also discovered a lot about good nutrition. This is a terrific fish dish that needs only some fresh steamed asparagus and brown rice to make it a full meal.

MUSTARD SAUCE

¼ cup Dijon mustard
2 teaspoons fresh lemon juice
2 teaspoons nonfat mayonnaise
2 teaspoons olive oil
1 clove garlic, crushed through a press
½ teaspoon black pepper
½ teaspoon paprika

PERCH

2 tablespoons olive oil
Four 6-ounce perch or snapper fillets
2 tablespoons low-sodium soy sauce
2 teaspoons fresh lemon juice
1 clove garlic, crushed through a press
½ teaspoon grated fresh ginger
½ teaspoon paprika
¼ teaspoon black pepper

To make the mustard sauce: In a small bowl, combine the mustard, lemon juice, mayonnaise, olive oil, garlic, pepper, and paprika. Stir until smooth. Set aside, covered, until ready to serve.

To prepare the fish: In a large nonstick skillet, heat the oil over medium heat. Add the fillets and cook for about 4 minutes, turning once, until the fish is lightly browned on both sides. Add the soy sauce, lemon juice, garlic, ginger, paprika, and pepper. Reduce the heat to low, cover, and simmer for 2 to 3 minutes, until the thickest part of the fillet is opaque when flaked with the tip of a sharp knife.

With a slotted spatula, transfer the fish to 4 dinner plates. Drizzle the cooking liquid evenly over the fish. Garnish with a dollop of the mustard sauce and serve immediately.

NUTRITIONAL CONTENT PER SERVING: **Calories: 169   Protein: 21 g**
Carbohydrates: 53 g   Fat: 16 g   Saturated fat: 2 g   Cholesterol: 48 mg
Sodium: 710 mg   Fiber: 5 g   30 percent calories from fat

Scallops with Red Pepper Sauce

Serves 3

When red bell peppers are roasted, they take on a wonderfully sweet, smoky flavor that tastes great with seafood. In this recipe I puree the roasted pepper and then mix it with sour cream substitute and garlic as a topping for bay scallops. This is excellent over pasta. Bay scallops are smaller than ocean scallops and often a little sweeter. If you cannot find them, use ocean scallops but cut them in halves or quarters to simulate little bay scallops.

1 large red bell pepper
1 tablespoon olive oil
12 ounces bay scallops
1 clove garlic, minced
1 cup nonfat sour cream substitute
¼ cup chopped scallions
⅛ teaspoon salt
⅛ teaspoon black pepper
8 ounces fettuccine

Position the broiler rack about 4 inches from the heat source and preheat the broiler. Broil the red pepper for about 10 minutes, turning occasionally, until the skin is blistered and blackened on all sides. Take the pepper from the broiler and drop it in a paper bag. Roll up the bag and let the pepper cool inside the bag. Using your hands, peel the charred skin from the pepper, and using a knife, scrape away the seeds. Put the seeded pepper in a blender or a food processor fitted with a metal blade and pulse until smooth. Set the pepper puree aside.

In a large nonstick skillet, heat the oil over medium-high heat. Add the scallops and garlic. Cook for about 5 minutes, turning occasionally, until the scallops are just opaque. Stir in the pepper puree, sour cream substitute, scallions, salt, and pepper. Cook just to heat through; do not boil.

Meanwhile, bring a large pot of lightly salted water to a boil; add the fettuccine and cook for about 9 minutes, until just tender. Drain well and place in a heated serving bowl. Add the scallops and sauce and toss well. Serve immediately.

NUTRITIONAL CONTENT PER SERVING: **Calories: 370   Protein: 26 g**
Carbohydrates: 52 g   Fat: 5 g   Saturated fat: 1 g   Cholesterol: 28 mg
Sodium: 236 mg   Fiber: 3 g   12 percent calories from fat

Fillet of Sole El Lupo

Lieutenant Wilfred "The Wolf" Schmelzinger
Engine Company 319
New York City Fire Department
Queens, New York

Serves 4

In most firehouses the lieutenants, captains, and chiefs leave the cooking to the firefighters, but "The Wolf" is the exception—not only does he love to work in the kitchen but he is a great cook! I worked with the lieutenant at Engine Company 319 before I transferred to Ladder Company 129 and found him to be one of the best fire officers on the job. This fast-cooking dish is one of his favorites, and because it is Italian in origin, we named it El Lupo—"The Wolf."

1 tablespoon olive oil
1 medium onion, finely chopped
1 cup crushed tomatoes
¾ cup dry Marsala wine
½ cup bottled clam juice
3 tablespoons finely chopped fresh parsley
⅛ teaspoon black pepper
Four 6-ounce sole or flounder fillets

In a large nonstick skillet, heat the oil over medium heat. Add the onion and cook for about 7 minutes, until it is golden. Stir in the tomatoes, Marsala wine, clam juice, parsley, and pepper and bring to a simmer.

Roll up the fillets to form thick cylinders. Place the fillets, seam side down, in the sauce. Cover and simmer for about 10 minutes, until the thickest part of the fish is opaque when flaked with the tip of a sharp knife.

With a slotted spatula, transfer the fillets to 4 dinner plates and spoon the sauce over the fish. Serve immediately.

NUTRITIONAL CONTENT PER SERVING: **Calories: 333   Protein: 44 g Carbohydrates: 12 g   Fat: 7 g   Saturated fat: 1 g   Cholesterol: 110 mg Sodium: 423 mg   Fiber: 2 g   17 percent calories from fat**

Cioppino

Mariann Landry

Serves 8

Secretary, Resources Management

Phoenix Fire Department

Phoenix, Arizona

This recipe comes from one of the most fitness-conscious departments in the country. The Phoenix FD organizes a health, fitness, and training seminar each year that attracts many fitness experts, as well as firefighters. This recipe, which comes from one of the fitness experts in the department, is part of a collection Mariann Landry put together for me.

1 tablespoon olive oil

1 large onion, chopped

1 green bell pepper, seeded and chopped

1 stalk celery, thinly sliced

2 cloves garlic, minced

One 28-ounce can peeled Italian tomatoes in thick puree

One 8-ounce can tomato sauce

1 cup dry vermouth or white wine

1 teaspoon dried basil

¼ teaspoon crushed hot red pepper flakes

1 pound cod or scrod fillets, cut in 1-inch pieces

½ pound medium shrimp, peeled and deveined

½ pound bay scallops

3 tablespoons chopped fresh parsley

In a Dutch oven, heat the oil over medium heat. Add the onion, green pepper, celery, and garlic. Cover and cook for about 5 minutes, stirring often, until the vegetables soften. Stir in the tomatoes with their puree, tomato sauce, vermouth, basil, and red pepper flakes. Bring to a simmer and reduce the heat to low. Simmer, uncovered, for about 45 minutes, until slightly thickened.

Add the cod or scrod and cook for 2 minutes. Add the shrimp and scallops and cook for about 3 minutes more, until all of the fish is opaque. Serve the cioppino in soup bowls, sprinkled with parsley.

NUTRITIONAL CONTENT PER SERVING: **Calories: 162   Protein: 23 g**

Carbohydrates: 11 g   Fat: 3 g   Saturated fat: 1 g   Cholesterol: 77 mg

Sodium: 529 mg   Fiber: 2 g   17 percent calories from fat

Johnny C's 32nd Street Kabobs

Firefighter John Caltagirone
Ladder Company 154
New York City Fire Department
Queens, New York

Serves 4

Kabobs are great in the summer when you're grilling outdoors. For these, do not put the cherry tomatoes on the skewers until the rest of the food is nearly cooked; otherwise, they will overcook and fall off the skewers. It's important to soak bamboo skewers for at least 30 minutes so that they won't smolder when set over the charcoal fire. You can also make these on metal skewers.

¼ cup prepared teriyaki sauce
¼ cup dry sherry
One 20-ounce can unsweetened pineapple chunks, juice reserved
1 clove garlic, minced
¼ teaspoon dry mustard
16 jumbo shrimp (about 1 pound), peeled and deveined
1 onion, quartered and separated
2 green bell peppers, seeded and cut in quarters
8 large whole mushrooms
8 cherry tomatoes

In a medium glass bowl, combine the teriyaki sauce, sherry, reserved pineapple juice, garlic, and mustard. Add the shrimp and toss well. Cover and refrigerate for at least 1 hour but no more than 2 hours.

Soak 4 long bamboo skewers in water for at least 30 minutes. Remove the shrimp from the marinade, reserving the marinade.

Thread the skewers with alternating shrimp, onion, green pepper, mushroom, and pineapple. Leave about 2 inches at the end of each skewer.

Build a medium-hot fire in a charcoal grill. Lightly oil the grill rack. Grill the shrimp kabobs for 4 minutes, brushing often with the reserved marinade. Carefully remove a kabob from the heat and put 2 cherry tomatoes on the end. Repeat the process with the remaining skewers. Return the kabobs to the grill and continue to grill and baste for about 4 more minutes, until the shrimp are pink and firm. Serve immediately.

NUTRITIONAL CONTENT PER SERVING: **Calories: 193   Protein: 18 g**
Carbohydrates: 25 g   Fat: 2 g   Saturated fat: 0 g   Cholesterol: 115 mg
Sodium: 167 mg   Fiber: 3 g   9 percent calories from fat

Cajun Seafood Gumbo

Firefighter Allison Hess

Serves 8

Metro-Dade Fire Department

Miami, Florida

Gumbo is associated more with Louisiana than with Florida, but the thick soup-stew is a classic regardless of where it is prepared. What distinguishes gumbo from other stews is that it is thickened with okra or filé powder and always starts with a thick flour base called a roux. Allison Hess, who has competed in the Florida Firefighter Olympics in power lifting and track, sent me this version of a healthful and tasty gumbo.

⅓ cup all-purpose flour
8⅓ cups chicken broth, preferably homemade (page 110), or canned
    low-sodium broth
1 tablespoon canola or other vegetable oil
2 large onions, chopped
1 large green bell pepper, seeded and chopped
1 stalk celery, chopped
5 cloves garlic, minced
8 ounces okra, cut in ½-inch pieces, or one 10-ounce package frozen okra,
    thawed
1 teaspoon dried thyme
1 teaspoon dried basil
2 bay leaves
½ teaspoon salt
¼ teaspoon ground red pepper

¼ teaspoon black pepper

1 pound medium shrimp, peeled and deveined

4 cups hot cooked rice

In a Dutch oven, combine the flour, ⅓ cup of the chicken broth, and the oil and whisk until smooth. Cook over medium heat for 10 to 15 minutes, whisking constantly, until the mixture turns a reddish brown.

Add the onions, green pepper, celery, and garlic. Continue to cook for about 5 minutes, stirring often, until the vegetables soften. Stir in the remaining 8 cups of chicken broth, the okra, thyme, basil, bay leaves, salt, ground red pepper, and black pepper. Bring to a simmer and reduce the heat to low. Simmer, uncovered, for about 30 minutes, until slightly thickened.

Add the shrimp and cook for about 3 minutes, until the shrimp are pink and firm. Serve the gumbo in soup bowls, topped with a spoonful of rice.

NUTRITIONAL CONTENT PER SERVING: **Calories: 272 Protein: 18 g**
Carbohydrates: 41 g Fat: 3 g Saturated fat: 1 g Cholesterol: 111 mg
Sodium: 401 mg Fiber: 3 g 11 percent calories from fat

Truckie's Shrimp Scampi

Firefighter Richard Curiel
Ladder Company 130
New York City Fire Department
Queens, New York

Serves 6

When too many firefighters are assigned to a tour of duty, one or two may be detailed to another firehouse for the tour. One night I was detailed to Ladder 130 and found myself partaking of a special meal. One of the firefighters was leaving for vacation the next day and so offered to make dinner. Rich cooked this scampi, and I was so impressed, I asked him for the recipe for the book. I thought it was superb and not in the least oily, as some scampi is. Plus, it tasted even better (I confess) because it was a "free" meal.

1½ pounds medium shrimp, peeled and deveined, shells reserved
3 cups chicken broth, preferably homemade (page 110), or canned
      low-sodium broth
2 bay leaves
½ teaspoon salt
¼ teaspoon black pepper
2 tablespoons olive oil
6 cloves garlic, minced
1½ teaspoons Italian herb seasoning
⅓ cup seasoned dried bread crumbs
1 pound spaghetti
2 tablespoons chopped fresh parsley

In a medium saucepan, bring the reserved shrimp shells, chicken broth, bay leaves, salt, and pepper to a boil over medium-high heat. Reduce the heat to low and simmer for 15 minutes. Strain and reserve the stock.

In a large skillet, heat the oil over medium heat. Add the garlic and cook for about 1 minute, stirring often, until it just turns golden. Add the shrimp and Italian seasoning. Cook for about 3 minutes, stirring often, until the shrimp just turn firm and pink. Transfer to a plate and set aside.

Add the reserved stock to the skillet and bring to a simmer over medium heat. Whisk in the bread crumbs to form a thin sauce. If necessary, add a few more bread crumbs or a little more water to get the proper consistency. Reduce the heat to low and simmer for 5 minutes, stirring often. Return the shrimp and garlic to the skillet and cook for about 1 minute, until the shrimp are just heated through. Do not overcook.

Meanwhile, bring a large pot of lightly salted water to a boil. Add the spaghetti and cook for about 9 minutes, until the pasta is just tender. Drain well and transfer to a warm serving bowl. Add the shrimp sauce and parsley, toss well, and serve immediately.

NUTRITIONAL CONTENT PER SERVING: **Calories: 759** **Protein: 56 g**
Carbohydrates: 110 g **Fat: 9 g** **Saturated fat: 1 g** **Cholesterol: 276 mg**
Sodium: 864 mg **Fiber: 6 g** **10 percent calories from fat**

Bayshore Crab Cakes

Firefighter Kenneth Eastman
Marine Company 1 Fire Boat
New York City Fire Department (Retired)

Makes 6 crab cakes

I have taken some liberties with Ken's original recipe for crab cakes, but the spirit of the recipe is the same: delicious patties full of crabmeat, augmented with bread crumbs, vegetables, and seasonings. To bind the ingredients, I use liquid egg substitute and nonfat mayonnaise, which make these crab cakes low in fat, calories, and cholesterol. It's important to use fresh crabmeat; canned just does not taste as good.

1 pound (about 2 cups) fresh crabmeat, picked over to remove cartilage
¼ cup nonfat mayonnaise
1 cup plain dried bread crumbs, divided
¼ cup liquid egg substitute
1 scallion, finely chopped
3 tablespoons finely chopped celery
2 tablespoons chopped fresh parsley
1 teaspoon Old Bay seasoning
1 teaspoon Worcestershire sauce
⅛ teaspoon black pepper
Lemon wedges

In a medium bowl, combine the crabmeat, mayonnaise, ¼ cup of the bread crumbs, liquid egg substitute, scallion, celery, parsley, Old Bay seasoning, Worcestershire sauce, and pepper. Cover and refrigerate for about 1 hour, until the mixture is chilled.

Line a baking sheet with waxed paper.

Remove the crab mixture from the refrigerator and form into 6 patties. Place the remaining bread crumbs on a plate. Coat each crab cake in the bread crumbs and pat to help the crumbs adhere. Place the breaded crab cakes on the prepared baking sheet and refrigerate for 30 minutes.

Spray a large nonstick skillet with nonstick cooking spray and heat over medium heat. Cook the crab cakes for about 5 minutes, turning once, until they are golden brown on both sides. Garnish with lemon wedges and serve immediately.

NUTRITIONAL CONTENT PER SERVING: **(1 serving = 1 crab cake)**
Calories: 248   Protein: 21 g   Carbohydrates: 28 g   Fat: 5 g   Saturated fat: 1 g
Cholesterol: 57 mg   Sodium: 780 mg   Fiber: 1 g   15 percent calories from fat

Fillet and Shrimp Roulades

New York City is surrounded by water, and many firefighters are avid fishermen on their time off. It's not unusual for a fellow firefighter to bring in some fresh fish after a few days of fishing for the night crew to clean and cook. This is just one example of a simple recipe for fresh fish—in this case, fillet of flounder or sole.

1 tablespoon olive oil
1 clove garlic, crushed through a press
1 small onion, minced
¼ cup minced green bell pepper
4 ounces medium shrimp, peeled, deveined, and coarsely chopped
¼ cup plain dried bread crumbs
2 tablespoons chopped fresh parsley, divided
1 tablespoon chopped fresh chives
¼ teaspoon salt
⅛ teaspoon black pepper
Four 8-ounce flounder or sole fillets
½ cup dry white wine

Preheat the oven to 350°F. Spray an 11-by-7-inch baking dish with nonstick cooking spray.

In a large nonstick skillet, heat the oil over medium heat. Add the garlic, onion, and green pepper. Cook for about 3 minutes, stirring often. Add the shrimp and continue to cook for about 2 minutes, until the shrimp are pink and the vegetables soften. Transfer to a bowl and stir in the bread crumbs, 1 tablespoon of the parsley, the chives, salt, and pepper.

Place a quarter of the mixture in the center of each fillet. Roll up each fillet to enclose the filling and secure each with a wooden toothpick. Lay the fillets, seamside down, in the prepared baking dish. Pour the wine over the fish.

Bake for about 25 minutes, basting occasionally, until the fish is opaque when flaked with the tip of a sharp knife. Sprinkle with the remaining parsley and serve immediately.

NUTRITIONAL CONTENT PER SERVING: **Calories: 208   Protein: 34 g Carbohydrates: 5 g   Fat: 5 g   Saturated fat: 1 g   Cholesterol: 119 mg Sodium: 305 mg   Fiber 1 g   21 percent calories from fat**

Stuffed Trout Montana

Firefighter Joseph Aquino and Debbie Aquino
Engine Company 42
New York City Fire Department
Bronx, New York (Retired to Montana)

Serves 6

Joe and I got to know each other when we were both appointed to the NYFD in May of 1979. Two years later, while searching for victims in a tenement filled with thick, acrid, black smoke, he fell five stories down an elevator shaft, sustaining massive injuries that ended his career. With a disability pension, Joe and his wife, Debbie, retired to Montana, where he spends his time hunting and fishing instead of fighting fires. Rainbow trout is plentiful in the mountain streams, and Joe shared this recipe for sweet freshwater fish with us. Everyone in the firehouse loves it—even though we usually have to get our trout from the local market.

¼ cup chicken broth, preferably homemade (page 110), or canned
    low-sodium broth
¼ cup dry white wine
½ cup chopped celery
½ cup finely chopped Granny Smith apple
½ cup chopped seeded orange
½ cup fresh or frozen cranberries
½ cup raisins
4 cups cubed whole wheat bread (about ½-inch pieces)
1 tablespoon poultry seasoning
1 tablespoon chopped fresh dill

2 cloves garlic, minced

½ teaspoon salt

½ teaspoon black pepper

6 rainbow trout, cleaned, with the undersides split lengthwise to form a pocket

Preheat the oven to 400°F. Lightly oil a 13-by-9-inch baking dish.

In a large skillet, bring the broth and wine to a simmer. Add the celery, apple, orange, cranberries, and raisins and cook for about 7 minutes, until the celery softens.

In a large bowl, combine the bread cubes, poultry seasoning, dill, garlic, salt, and pepper. Add the fruit mixture and toss well to combine. Stuff each trout with about ½ cup of the fruit-bread mixture.

Put the stuffed trout into the prepared baking dish. Sprinkle the remaining bread mixture on top of the fish. Bake for about 20 minutes, until the fish are opaque when flaked with the tip of a sharp knife. Serve immediately.

NUTRITIONAL CONTENT PER SERVING: **Calories: 328   Protein: 34 g**
Carbohydrates: 34 g   Fat: 6 g   Saturated fat: 1 g   Cholesterol: 84 mg
Sodium: 195 mg   Fiber: 5 g   17 percent calories from fat

Scallops, Asparagus, and Pasta à la Murphy

Firefighter Shawn Murphy

Serves 6

Ladder Company 129

New York City Fire Department

Flushing, New York

Shawn is one of the best cooks in the firehouse, and so when he cooks, it is always a treat. He is also an excellent athlete and believes in eating well to help keep in shape for the NYFD boxing team. He explains that asparagus is a good source of beta carotene, vitamins B and C, and potassium and produces an alkaloid called asparagine, which purifies the blood and soothes the central nervous system—all reasons why he came up with this recipe in the first place. It tastes fantastic too.

1 tablespoon olive oil

6 cloves garlic, chopped

1 small onion, thinly sliced

1 to 1½ pounds asparagus, peeled if necessary and cut in ½-inch pieces

8 plum tomatoes, seeded and chopped

1 teaspoon dried basil

¼ teaspoon salt

⅛ teaspoon black pepper

½ cup dry white wine

1½ pounds bay scallops

1 pound farfalle (bow tie) pasta

6 tablespoons grated Parmesan cheese

In a large nonstick skillet, heat the oil over medium heat. Add the garlic and cook for about 1 minute, stirring often, until it is barely golden. Add the onion, asparagus, tomatoes, basil, salt, and pepper. Cover and cook for about 5 minutes, stirring often, until the asparagus are crisp-tender. Add the wine and simmer, uncovered, for about 1 minute. Add the scallops and cook for about 5 minutes, stirring occasionally, until they are firm and opaque.

Meanwhile, bring a large pot of lightly salted water to a boil. Add the pasta and cook for about 9 minutes, until the pasta is just tender. Drain well and transfer to a warm serving bowl. Add the scallop mixture, toss well, and serve immediately. Pass the Parmesan cheese at the table.

NUTRITIONAL CONTENT PER SERVING: **Calories: 469   Protein: 32 g   Carbohydrates: 68 g   Fat: 7 g   Saturated fat: 1 g   Cholesterol: 38 mg   Sodium: 252 mg   Fiber: 6 g   14 percent calories from fat**

Bobby's Tuna Chowder

Robert Bonanno
North Babylon, New York

Serves 8

Bobby may not be a firefighter, but he's related to a few, so I think he qualifies to be in this book. You can make this chowder in the dead of winter when the only fresh vegetables you can find are onions, carrots, and celery. And canned tuna is available all year long. Trust my brother to come up with a great, easy recipe.

1 tablespoon canola or other vegetable oil
1 chopped onion
1 large carrot, thinly sliced
2 stalks celery, thinly sliced
2 boiling potatoes, peeled and sliced ½ inch thick
2 cloves garlic, minced
2 cups chicken broth, preferably homemade (page 110), or canned
    low-sodium broth
1 teaspoon dried thyme
2 tablespoons chopped fresh parsley
¼ teaspoon salt
¼ teaspoon black pepper
6 cups skim milk
Two 6⅛-ounce cans water-packed solid white tuna, drained

In a large soup pot, heat the oil over medium heat. Add the onion, carrot, celery, potatoes, and garlic. Cook for about 2 minutes, stirring constantly, until the onion begins to soften.

Add the chicken broth, thyme, parsley, salt, and pepper and bring to a boil. Reduce the heat to low, cover, and simmer for about 15 minutes, until the potatoes are just tender.

With a slotted spoon, transfer about 2 cups of the vegetables with about ½ cup of the cooking liquid to a blender and process until smooth, adding more liquid if necessary to achieve a good consistency. Stir the pureed vegetables back into the pot. Stir in the milk and tuna and heat just to a simmer; do not boil. Serve immediately.

NUTRITIONAL CONTENT PER SERVING: **Calories: 204   Protein: 19 g**
Carbohydrates: 29 g   Fat: 1 g   Saturated fat: 0 g   Cholesterol: 9 mg
Sodium: 271 mg   Fiber: 2 g   4 percent calories from fat

Dilled Shrimp Pilaf

The combination of dill and shrimp is one of the best. Here I use it in a rice dish that you can prepare in less than an hour.

2 tablespoons olive oil, divided
1 pound medium shrimp, peeled and deveined
1 stalk celery, finely chopped
1 scallion, finely chopped
1 cup long-grain white rice
2½ cups chicken broth, preferably homemade (page 110), or canned
    low-sodium broth
1 tablespoon chopped fresh dill
¼ teaspoon black pepper

In a large nonstick skillet, heat 1 tablespoon of the oil over medium heat. Add the shrimp and cook for about 3 minutes, stirring often, until they are pink and firm. Transfer to a plate and set aside.

Add the remaining 1 tablespoon of oil to the skillet and heat over medium heat. Add the celery and scallion, cover, and cook for about 3 minutes, until the celery begins to soften. Stir in the rice and cook for about 2 minutes, stirring constantly, until it turns opaque. Stir in the chicken broth, dill, salt, and pepper. Bring to a simmer and reduce the heat to low. Cover and simmer for 15 to 20 minutes, until the rice is tender and the liquid is absorbed.

Stir in the shrimp and cook for about 1 minute, stirring often, until the shrimp are just reheated. Serve immediately.

NUTRITIONAL CONTENT PER SERVING: **Calories: 376   Protein: 30 g**

Carbohydrates: 39 g   Fat: 10 g   Saturated fat: 2 g   Cholesterol: 172 mg

Sodium: 935 mg   Fiber: 1 g   25 percent calories from fat

Orange-Glazed Halibut

Firefighter Joseph Aquino and Debbie Aquino   Serves 4
Engine Company 42
New York City Fire Department
Bronx, New York (Retired to Montana)

Here is another great fish recipe from my friends in Montana. The
cornstarch thickens the sauce just enough so that the orange juice glazes it
as it bakes.

1 tablespoon butter
1 scallion, finely chopped
4 teaspoons cornstarch
1 cup orange juice
½ cup chicken broth, preferably homemade (page 110), or canned
     low-sodium broth
Four 8-ounce halibut or cod steaks, about ¾ inch thick
1 orange, peeled and cut crosswise into 4 slices

continued

Preheat the oven to 350°F. Choose a shallow baking dish large enough to hold the fish in one layer and spray it with nonstick cooking spray.

In a small saucepan, melt the butter over medium heat. Add the scallion and cook for about 1 minute, stirring often, until it softens.

In a small bowl, whisk the cornstarch into the orange juice and chicken broth until it is dissolved. Pour the mixture into the saucepan and cook for about 2 minutes, until the sauce is simmering and thickened.

Arrange the halibut or cod in the prepared dish. Place an orange slice on top of each fish steak. Pour the sauce over the fish and bake for about 20 minutes, until the fish is opaque when flaked with the tip of a knife. Serve immediately.

NUTRITIONAL CONTENT PER SERVING: **Calories: 182 Protein: 24 g
Carbohydrates: 9 g Fat: 5 g Saturated fat: 1 g Cholesterol: 36 mg
Sodium: 273 mg Fiber: 1 g 24 percent calories from fat**

Shrimp and Lima Bean Casserole

Serves 4

You may never have thought of combining lima beans with shrimp, but try it—you'll like it. Like all beans, limas are a good source of B vitamins and fiber.

    1 tablespoon canola or other vegetable oil
    1 tablespoon butter
    12 ounces medium shrimp, peeled and deveined

⅓ cup finely chopped onion

⅓ cup chopped celery

⅓ cup finely chopped red bell pepper

3 tablespoons all-purpose flour

1½ teaspoons curry powder

½ teaspoon salt

⅛ teaspoon black pepper

1¾ cups skim milk

One 12-ounce package frozen lima beans, thawed

⅓ cup fresh bread crumbs

Preheat the oven to 350°F. Spray the inside of a 2-quart baking dish with nonstick cooking spray.

In a large nonstick skillet, heat the oil and butter over medium heat. Add the shrimp, onion, celery, and red pepper. Cook for about 3 minutes, stirring often, until the shrimp are pink and firm. Sprinkle with the flour, curry powder, salt, and pepper and cook for 1 minute longer, stirring constantly. Gradually add the milk and stir for about 2 minutes, until the mixture comes to a simmer and thickens.

Pour the mixture into the prepared baking dish. Stir in the lima beans and sprinkle with the bread crumbs. Bake for about 15 minutes, until the casserole is bubbling and the top is browned. Serve immediately.

NUTRITIONAL CONTENT PER SERVING: **Calories: 279   Protein: 23 g Carbohydrates: 33 g   Fat: 6 g   Saturated fat: 1 g   Cholesterol: 88 mg Sodium: 696 mg   Fiber: 10 g   18 percent calories from fat**

Mussels LaClair

Firefighter Kevin LaClair and Stephanie LaClair

Ladder Company 129

New York City Fire Department

Flushing, New York

Serves 6

Mussels are one of the most overlooked bivalves in the fish market, but the fact is they are inexpensive, low in fat, and high in protein, and they taste awfully good. Most mussels sold nowadays are farmed, or cultivated, specimens that are raised in clean seawater. When you get mussels home, hold them under cool running water and use a firm brush to scrub them clean and remove their "beards"—bristly fibers extending from between the shells. Soaking them for about an hour in cold water helps rid them of excess sand too.

5 pounds mussels, debearded and scrubbed

½ teaspoon coarsely ground black pepper

2 tablespoons olive oil

1 onion, chopped

4 cloves garlic, or more to taste, chopped

2 cups dry white wine

One 28-ounce can peeled Italian plum tomatoes, drained and chopped

¼ cup chopped fresh basil

¼ cup chopped fresh parsley

½ teaspoon crushed hot red pepper flakes

In a large soup pot, cover the mussels with cold water. Stir in the pepper. Let stand for 1 hour to let the mussels disgorge any sand. Drain, rinse, and drain again.

Rinse and dry the soup pot and heat the oil in it over medium heat. Add the onion and garlic and cook for about 4 minutes, stirring often, until the onion softens. Stir in the wine, tomatoes, basil, parsley, and red pepper flakes. Cook for about 5 minutes, until the liquid is slightly evaporated.

Add the mussels, cover, and cook for 8 to 10 minutes, until the mussels have opened. Discard any that do not open. Ladle the mussels and sauce into soup bowls and serve immediately.

NUTRITIONAL CONTENT PER SERVING: **Calories: 205   Protein: 15 g**
Carbohydrates: 11 g   Fat: 8 g   Saturated fat: 1 g   Cholesterol: 32 mg
Sodium: 529 mg   Fiber: 2 g   36 percent calories from fat

Asian Grilled Swordfish Steaks

Firefighter Christopher Schulte

USS *Capodanno*, E Division

U.S. Navy

Serves 4

When I received this recipe from Christopher Schulte, it called for shark steaks rather than swordfish. I altered it mainly because shark is not readily available in most fish markets and swordfish is. If you have access to shark, by all means try it. Tuna would also be good prepared this way.

⅓ cup pineapple juice
¼ cup red wine
1 tablespoon soy sauce
2 teaspoons brown sugar
½ teaspoon ground ginger
½ teaspoon dry mustard
1 clove garlic, crushed through a press
Four 8-ounce swordfish steaks, about ¾ inch thick

In a shallow glass dish, combine the pineapple juice, red wine, soy sauce, brown sugar, ginger, mustard, and garlic and stir until the sugar dissolves. Add the swordfish, cover, and refrigerate for at least 2 hours but not longer than 4 hours. Turn occasionally.

Meanwhile, build a hot fire in a charcoal grill or heat a gas grill to high heat. Lightly oil a grill rack.

Remove the swordfish from the marinade, reserving the marinade. Place the steaks on the grill and cook for 8 to 10 minutes, turning once, until the fish

 The Healthy Firehouse Cookbook

appears slightly translucent in the center when cut with the tip of a sharp knife. Brush often with the reserved marinade. This will produce medium-rare swordfish steaks; continue grilling if you prefer more well-done fish. Serve immediately.

NUTRITIONAL CONTENT PER SERVING: **Calories: 168   Protein: 16 g Carbohydrates: 17 g   Fat: 4 g   Saturated fat: 1 g   Cholesterol: 35 mg Sodium: 319 mg   Fiber: 2 g   19 percent calories from fat**

Cajun Smoked Catfish

Firefighter Michael Bonanno

Serves 8

Ladder Company 7

New York City Fire Department

New York, New York

Liquid Smoke adds a wonderful flavor to catfish, and Cajun seasoning spices them up even more. Mild, farm-raised catfish is the perfect foil for these strong flavors. This recipe is from my youngest brother, Michael, who loves to stay in shape so he can compete in the New York City Marathon and in corporate-sponsored stair-climbing races, which are vertical runs up the stairwells of some of the city's tallest skyscrapers. As they say, only in New York! Michael has been assigned to companies in Brooklyn and Queens, but prefers Manhattan.

Six 8-ounce catfish fillets
2 teaspoons Liquid Smoke flavoring
2 tablespoons Cajun seasoning
1 tablespoon olive oil
Lime wedges

Sprinkle both sides of the catfish fillets with the Liquid Smoke and then the Cajun seasoning.

In a large nonstick skillet, heat the oil over medium heat. Cook the catfish for about 5 minutes, turning once, until the fish is opaque when flaked with the tip of a sharp knife. Garnish with the lime wedges and serve immediately.

NUTRITIONAL CONTENT PER SERVING: **Calories: 419   Protein: 44 g**

Carbohydrates: 29 g   Fat: 12 g   Saturated fat: 3 g   Cholesterol: 132 mg

Sodium: 498 mg   Fiber: 1 g   27 percent calories from fat

Poultry and Meat

Chicken Joseph

Chief Joseph Gilbert

Serves 8

New Orleans Fire Department

New Orleans, Louisiana

This great idea for chicken and stuffing comes from a fellow firefighter in Louisiana, where rice plays an important role in the everyday diet. Instead of a bread-based stuffing, this chicken is stuffed with a rice-based mixture. I suggest using turkey sausage instead of the more traditional pork sausage to save on fat and calories.

3 cups water

¾ teaspoon salt, divided

1½ cups rice

12 ounces Italian turkey sausage, casings removed and roughly chopped

1 small onion, chopped

1 small green bell pepper, seeded and finely chopped

2 cloves garlic, minced

1 shallot or scallion, minced

One 5½- to 6-pound chicken

1 slice whole wheat bread

1 tablespoon olive oil

⅛ teaspoon black pepper

Preheat the oven to 350°F.

In a medium saucepan, bring the water and ½ teaspoon salt to a boil over medium heat. Stir in the rice. Cover, reduce the heat to low, and simmer for 15 to 18 minutes, until the rice is just tender.

In a nonstick skillet, cook the sausage, onion, green pepper, garlic, and shallot over medium heat for about 8 minutes, until the sausage is cooked through, stirring often to break up the sausage. Stir in the rice.

Fill the chicken cavity with the rice-sausage mixture and tuck the slice of bread into the opening to keep the stuffing inside.

Brush the chicken with the olive oil and sprinkle it with the remaining ¼ teaspoon salt and the black pepper.

Place the chicken on a rack in a roasting pan, breast side down, and roast for 1 hour, basting occasionally with the pan juices. Turn the chicken breast side up and roast for about 40 minutes more, until a meat thermometer inserted in the thigh reads 170°F.

Transfer the chicken to a serving plate and let it stand for 5 minutes before carving.

Skim as much fat as possible from the pan juices, then pour the juices into a deep, heat-resistant container. Let cool slightly and skim off the fat that rises to the surface. Serve the chicken hot with the pan juices.

NUTRITIONAL CONTENT PER SERVING: **Calories: 534   Protein: 42 g**
Carbohydrates: 47 g   Fat: 18 g   Saturated fat: 6 g   Cholesterol: 120 mg
Sodium: 471 mg   Fiber 2 g   31 percent calories from fat

Easy Chicken-Broccoli Stir-fry

Firefighter Wade R. Abbott

Tateville Volunteer Fire Department

Tateville, Kentucky

Serves 4

The trick to stir-frying is to make sure the pan is hot enough and to cook the food in the correct order so that everything is properly done at the same time. Having the pan nice and hot also ensures that the oil will be hot enough to keep it from being absorbed by the food.

1 bunch broccoli, cut into florets, stems trimmed and sliced ½ inch thick

⅔ cup cold chicken broth, preferably homemade (page 110), or canned low-sodium broth

2 tablespoons low-sodium soy sauce

1 tablespoon cornstarch

2 tablespoons canola or other vegetable oil

1 scallion, finely chopped

1 clove garlic, finely chopped

2 teaspoons grated fresh ginger

1 pound skinless, boneless chicken breast, cut into 1-inch strips

2 cups hot cooked rice

In a large saucepan of lightly salted water, cook the broccoli stems for 2 minutes. Add the florets and cook for about 2 more minutes, until the broccoli is barely tender. Drain, rinse under cold water, and drain again.

In a small bowl, combine the broth and soy sauce. Whisk in the cornstarch until it is dissolved.

Preheat a large skillet or wok over high heat and add the oil. When hot, add the scallion, garlic, and ginger and stir-fry for 30 seconds. Add the chicken and stir-fry for about 3 minutes, until it is just firm and opaque. Add the broccoli and stir-fry for 1 minute.

Stir in the cornstarch mixture. Cook and stir for about 1 minute, until thickened and bubbly. Serve immediately over the rice.

NUTRITIONAL CONTENT PER SERVING: **Calories: 343   Protein: 26 g**
Carbohydrates: 37 g   Fat: 10 g   Saturated fat: 1 g   Cholesterol: 58 mg
Sodium: 328 mg   Fiber: 3 g   26 percent calories from fat

Italian Grilled Chicken

Firefighter Bob Turk
Engine Company 72
Westlake Fire Department
Westlake, Ohio

Serves 4

The most fat-laden part of the chicken (or any poultry) is the skin. Once it is removed, the chicken is far more healthy, and the fat content drops to close to nothing. Don't use the marinade as a basting sauce during cooking because it might contain harmful bacteria absorbed from the chicken during marinating.

continued

Four 5-ounce skinless, boneless chicken breasts
¾ cup prepared nonfat Italian dressing
2 tablespoons low-sodium soy sauce
1 tablespoon dried oregano

Lay the chicken breasts between 2 sheets of moistened waxed paper and, using a meat mallet, pound the chicken to flatten it slightly.

In a shallow nonaluminum dish, mix the dressing, soy sauce, and oregano. Put the flattened chicken breasts into the liquid. Cover and refrigerate for at least 1 hour and up to 4 hours, turning the chicken several times.

Preheat the broiler or gas grill or build a medium-hot fire in a charcoal grill. Remove the chicken from the marinade and discard the marinade.

Broil or grill the chicken for 3 to 4 minutes per side, until the meat feels firm when pressed with a finger. Serve immediately.

NUTRITIONAL CONTENT PER SERVING: **Calories: 195   Protein: 27 g**
Carbohydrates: 9 g   Fat: 3 g   Saturated fat: 1 g   Cholesterol: 73 mg
Sodium: 2,001 mg   Fiber: 1 g   15 percent calories from fat

Oven Roaster Ready

New York has the busiest fire department in the world. Every year more than 2 million fires are reported in the United States and 100,000 of those occur in New York City. The firefighters that make up its uniformed force are aptly nicknamed "The Bravest." They regularly risk life and limb to protect New York's citizens under often intolerable conditions. Some of the fiercest fires take place in East New York, a Brooklyn neighborhood where blazes are often the work of arsonists.

My old engine company "interchanged" regularly with a busier engine company in East New York, where the ghetto firefighters are recognized as the toughest of the tough. One night I helped prepare the evening meal, simple oven-stuffer roasting chickens with rice and broccoli. One of the firefighters from the regular Brooklyn company pulled out those pop-up timers in the chickens and handed one to each of us. I was fairly new on the job and shyly asked what I should do with it. He said to put it in the headband of my helmet and explained that it is a good indicator of when to get out of a fire. My cooking experience told me that for those timers to "pop," the temperature has to reach 350°F and stay there for at least an hour.

We had just put our forks into our meal when an alarm rang. From blocks away, the blazing summer fire glowed orange against the dark Brooklyn sky. Upon arriving at the fire, I donned my gear, pulled off a length of hose, and disappeared with my fellow firefighters into a burning building.

We returned to quarters past midnight, exhausted and starving. We ate ravenously, and while cleaning up, I remembered the pop-up timers. The veteran firefighter fetched our helmets, and we compared them. Not only had the pop-up timers popped, but they were almost completely melted. By all indications, we had been in extreme conditions. I guess for chickens or firefighters, it was a job "well done."

Spinach Turkey Roll

Firefighter John Smilnak
Livenia Firefighters Safety Committee
Livenia, Michigan

Serves 6

This recipe may seem fussy because you have to roll the ground turkey into a cylinder. But foil helps you form the roll easily, and once the roll is cooked and cooled slightly, it slices very nicely. Be sure to wash your hands before mixing the turkey and again before spreading it into a rectangle. Raw poultry can contain salmonella bacteria, and it's advisable to wash your hands and all work surfaces and utensils with warm soap and water when working with it. Be sure to wash up before working with other food, even in the same recipe. Thorough cooking kills any bacteria in the meat.

2 pounds ground turkey
1 small onion, finely chopped
1 cup tomato sauce, divided
½ cup fresh whole wheat bread crumbs (about 2 slices)
4 large egg whites, slightly beaten, or ½ cup liquid egg substitute
1½ teaspoons dry mustard
½ teaspoon salt
1 teaspoon dried oregano
1 clove garlic, crushed through a press
One 10-ounce package frozen chopped spinach, thawed and squeezed dry
4 ounces part-skim mozzarella cheese, shredded (about 1 cup)

Preheat the oven to 350°F. Lightly oil an 18-by-15-inch sheet of foil.

In a large bowl, combine the turkey, onion, ¼ cup of the tomato sauce, the bread crumbs, egg whites, mustard, salt, oregano, and garlic. Mix thoroughly by hand.

Put the turkey mixture on top of the foil and form a 12-by-8-inch rectangle. Spread the spinach over the turkey and then sprinkle about three fourths of the cheese on top. Lift up the foil on the shorter side and, using it as a guide, roll the turkey, jelly-roll fashion, into a cylinder.

Lightly oil a baking sheet and lay the foil-wrapped turkey roll, seam side down, on it. Bake for about 50 minutes, until a meat thermometer inserted into the center of the roll reads 160°F. Remove the pan from the oven and carefully pour off any fat that has accumulated in the pan.

Unwrap the turkey roll, leaving it lying on the foil. Pour the remaining tomato sauce over the top of the roll and sprinkle with the remaining cheese. Return it, unwrapped, to the oven and bake for about 10 more minutes, until the cheese melts. Remove the roll from the oven, let stand for 5 minutes, and then slice and serve.

NUTRITIONAL CONTENT PER SERVING: **Calories: 286   Protein: 40 g**
Carbohydrates: 14 g   Fat: 8 g   Saturated fat: 4 g   Cholesterol: 165 mg
Sodium: 727 mg   Fiber: 3 g   25 percent calories from fat

Enzo's Power Loaf

Firefighter Steven Fernandes
Engine Company 3
Linden Fire Department
Linden, New Jersey

Serves 6

This recipe is similar to the preceding one, in that you roll the ground turkey into a cylinder and bake it. This one is rolled around beta carotene-rich broccoli. Be sure to wash your hands, work surfaces, and utensils with warm soapy water before and after working with raw poultry.

2 cups broccoli florets
1 cup vegetable juice (such as V-8) or tomato juice
¾ cup rolled oats
2 large egg whites
2 cloves garlic, crushed through a press
½ teaspoon dried oregano
½ teaspoon dried basil
½ teaspoon salt
½ teaspoon black pepper
1½ pounds ground turkey

In a large pot of boiling lightly salted water, cook the broccoli for about 6 minutes, until it is quite tender. Drain, rinse under cold water, and drain again well. With either a food processor or a sharp knife, finely chop the broccoli. Then, in as many batches as necessary, squeeze the chopped broccoli in a clean kitchen towel to remove excess liquid. Set the broccoli aside.

Preheat the oven to 350°F and lightly oil a baking sheet. Lightly oil an 18-by-15-inch sheet of aluminum foil and lay it on the baking sheet.

In a large bowl, stir together the juice, oats, egg whites, garlic, oregano, basil, salt, and pepper. Add the turkey and mix well by hand. Turn out the mixture onto the sheet of aluminum foil and pat it into a 12-by-10-inch rectangle.

Spread the chopped broccoli over the surface of the turkey, leaving a 1-inch border on all sides. Then, starting at a short end and using the foil as an aid, roll up the turkey, jelly-roll fashion, into a cylinder.

Put the foil-wrapped turkey loaf seam side down on the baking sheet. Bake for 1 to 1¼ hours, until a meat thermometer inserted in the center of the loaf reads 165°F. Remove the roll from the oven and let stand for about 15 minutes, then unwrap, slice, and serve.

NUTRITIONAL CONTENT PER SERVING: **Calories: 144** **Protein: 18 g**
Carbohydrates: 12 g **Fat: 3 g** **Saturated fat: 1 g** **Cholesterol: 34 mg**
Sodium: 378 mg **Fiber: 3 g** **19 percent calories from fat**

Bruni Chicken

Firefighter Joseph Bruni

Master Station

St. Petersburg Fire Department

St. Petersburg, Florida

Serves 2

This dish may seem a little fancy for a firehouse meal, but I wanted to include it because it tastes so good and is so easy to make. The spinach is an excellent source of vitamins and iron and, with the apricots, provides beta carotene. This is a simple, elegant supper to have at home.

2 tablespoons whole wheat or all-purpose flour

1 cup chicken broth, preferably homemade (page 110), or canned
    low-sodium broth

2 tablespoons honey

⅓ cup fresh lemon juice

1 teaspoon poultry seasoning

1 teaspoon dried oregano

1 teaspoon dried basil

Two 4-ounce skinless, boneless chicken breast halves

1 pound fresh spinach, well washed, stems removed, and cut into ½-inch
    strips

One 15-ounce can unsweetened apricot halves, drained

In a nonstick skillet, whisk the flour with ⅓ cup of the chicken broth to make a paste. Whisk in the remaining broth and the honey. Cook over low heat for about 4 minutes, whisking constantly, until the sauce is smooth and thickened. Stir in the lemon juice, poultry seasoning, oregano, and basil.

Arrange the chicken breasts in the sauce. Bring them to a simmer, reduce the heat to low, and gently cook, covered, for about 15 minutes, until the chicken is firm.

Place the spinach on a serving platter. Set the chicken on top of the spinach and pour some of the sauce over it. Pour the remaining sauce into a sauceboat. Arrange the apricot halves around the chicken on top of the spinach. Serve immediately; pass the sauce at the table.

NUTRITIONAL CONTENT PER SERVING: **Calories: 368   Protein: 36 g
Carbohydrates: 51 g   Fat: 5 g   Saturated fat: 1 g   Cholesterol: 73 mg
Sodium: 910 mg   Fiber: 8 g   11 percent calories from fat**

Fusaro's Famous Stuffed Chicken

Firefighter Christopher Fusaro

Serves 4

Engine Company 273

New York Fire Department

Flushing, New York

Chris is another example of a dedicated firefighter. In his off time, he is a commissioner of the Huntington Manor Volunteer Fire Department on Long Island. He likes to cook at the firehouse, and I know his colleagues look forward to his meals. This stuffed chicken breast is one of his classic offerings. There's not a firefighter in Engine Company 273 who will not recognize this dish.

Four 5-ounce skinless, boneless chicken breast halves
One 10-ounce package frozen chopped spinach, thawed and squeezed dry
2 ounces feta cheese, crumbled (about 2 tablespoons)
1 clove garlic, crushed through a press
⅛ teaspoon salt
⅛ teaspoon black pepper
1 large egg white
2 tablespoons skim milk
1 cup dried seasoned bread crumbs
2 ounces part-skim mozzarella cheese, shredded (about ½ cup)
One 10¾-ounce can 99-percent-fat-free cream of chicken soup
⅔ cup water

Preheat the oven to 375°F. Spray a baking sheet with nonstick cooking spray.

Using a thin, sharp knife, cut each chicken breast horizontally into 2 thin slices.

In a medium bowl, mix the spinach, feta cheese, garlic, salt, and pepper.

Place a quarter of the spinach mixture on a slice of the chicken, leaving a border around the edges. Top the chicken with another slice of chicken and press the edges together. Repeat the process with the remaining chicken breast slices and spinach stuffing.

In a shallow dish, whisk the egg white and milk. Spread the bread crumbs in another shallow bowl. Dip the stuffed chicken breasts into the egg mixture and then into the bread crumbs. Pat to help the crumbs adhere.

Lay the breaded chicken breasts on the baking sheet. Bake for about 20 minutes; turn and bake for about 20 more minutes, until the chicken is golden brown. During the last 5 minutes of baking, sprinkle with the mozzarella cheese.

Meanwhile, in a medium saucepan, combine the soup and water. Bring to a simmer over medium heat to form a sauce; keep warm. Serve the stuffed chicken breasts with the warm sauce.

NUTRITIONAL CONTENT PER SERVING: **Calories: 480   Protein: 415 g Carbohydrates: 31 g   Fat: 11 g   Saturated fat: 5 g   Cholesterol: 100 mg Sodium: 1,426 mg   Fiber: 2 g   21 percent calories from fat**

Robin's Curry-Crust Chicken

Robin and Ranier Hartmann
Counselors, Muscle and Fitness Camp
Los Angeles, California

Serves 2

Because I am interested in physical fitness and training, I attended the Muscle and Fitness Camp in California run by Dr. Thomas Deters, editor-in-chief of *Muscle and Fitness Magazine.* I learned more in five days at camp than I had learned anywhere else and was impressed by the wealth of information on bodybuilding, fitness, and nutrition provided by Dr. Deters and his excellent staff. We were introduced to celebrity guests at training seminars, including Lou Ferrigno, "The Incredible Hulk" of television fame. This is a quick and easy bodybuilding recipe from two of the finest counselors at the camp.

1 cup crumbled shredded wheat cereal
2 large egg whites, lightly beaten
1¼ teaspoons garlic powder
½ teaspoon curry powder
1¼ teaspoons black pepper
Two 4-ounce skinless, boneless chicken breast halves
1 teaspoon Asian sesame oil
¼ cup prepared chutney

Put the crumbled shredded wheat in a shallow bowl. In a medium bowl, combine the egg whites, garlic powder, curry powder, and pepper.

Dip the chicken breasts into the spiced egg mixture and then into the shredded wheat crumbs. Pat to help the crumbs adhere to the chicken.

In a large nonstick skillet, heat the oil over medium heat. Cook the chicken for about 3 minutes; turn and cook for about 3 minutes more, until the chicken is firm. Serve immediately with the chutney.

NUTRITIONAL CONTENT PER SERVING: **Calories: 258   Protein: 33 g
Carbohydrates: 18 g   Fat: 6 g   Saturated fat: 1 g   Cholesterol: 73 mg
Sodium: 121 mg   Fiber: 3 g   21 percent calories from fat**

Broccoli Chicken Roll

Serves 6

This is one of my favorites to make at the firehouse because it always turns out perfectly. It's easy to prepare but appears elegant and makes the cook look grand. The firefighters in my company like it as a change from stews and chilies, and the cheese makes it plenty filling.

½ cup finely chopped shallots or scallions
1 pound mushrooms, sliced
2 tablespoons dry sherry
2 cups chopped broccoli florets
2 ounces low-fat Swiss cheese, shredded (about ½ cup), divided
2 tablespoons grated Parmesan cheese
Six 5-ounce skinless, boneless chicken breast halves
¼ teaspoon salt
⅛ teaspoon black pepper

Preheat the oven to 375°F.

Spray a large nonstick skillet with nonstick cooking spray and heat over medium heat. Add the shallots, mushrooms, and sherry, cover, and cook for about 5 minutes, until the mushrooms are soft. Add the broccoli, cover, and cook for about 7 minutes, stirring occasionally, until the broccoli is tender-crisp. Remove from the heat and stir in ¼ cup of the Swiss cheese, and the Parmesan cheese. Let cool.

Lay the chicken between 2 sheets of moistened waxed paper and, with a meat mallet, pound the chicken breasts until they are ⅛ inch thick.

Divide the broccoli mixture into 6 equal portions and mound a portion in the center of each chicken breast.

Spray a baking sheet with nonstick cooking spray. Roll the edges of the chicken breasts around the filling and set each roll, seam side down, on the baking sheet. Bake, uncovered, for about 30 minutes, until the meat is no longer pink and the filling is hot. Cut one to test.

Remove the baking sheet from the oven. Position the broiling rack 4 inches from the heat source and preheat the broiler. Sprinkle the remaining Swiss cheese on the chicken rolls and broil for about 2 minutes, until the cheese is golden brown. Serve immediately.

NUTRITIONAL CONTENT PER SERVING: **Calories: 243   Protein: 34 g Carbohydrates: 7 g   Fat: 8 g   Saturated fat: 3 g   Cholesterol: 78 mg Sodium: 142 mg   Fiber: 2 g   30 percent calories from fat**

Firehouse Chicken 'n' Dumplings

When I make chicken and dumplings at the firehouse, the other firefighters come running. Cooking in the microwave makes this dish fast and simple, and because the chicken is cut into relatively small pieces, it cooks evenly in a short amount of time.

1½ cups flour, divided
2 pounds skinless, boneless chicken thighs, cut into 2-inch pieces
1 tablespoon canola or other vegetable oil
1 tablespoon butter
3 medium leeks, white part only, halved and thinly sliced
3 medium carrots, thinly sliced
1 cup chicken broth, preferably homemade (page 110), or canned
    low-sodium broth, divided
½ cup apple juice
1 bay leaf
½ teaspoon dried thyme
2 teaspoons baking powder
½ teaspoon salt, divided
2 tablespoons chopped fresh parsley
¾ cup evaporated skim milk
1 cup fresh or thawed frozen peas
⅛ teaspoon black pepper

Put ¼ cup of the flour in a shallow dish. Dredge the chicken in the flour and shake off the excess.

In a large skillet, heat the oil and butter over medium-high heat. In as many batches as necessary, cook the chicken for about 4 minutes, turning to brown it lightly on all sides. Transfer the chicken to a plate and set aside.

Stir the leeks, carrots, and ½ cup of the chicken broth into the skillet. Cook over medium heat for about 3 minutes, stirring often, until the liquid is almost evaporated. Scrape the leek mixture into a microwave-safe 3-quart casserole and add the chicken pieces with their juices, the remaining ½ cup broth, and the apple juice, bay leaf, and thyme. Cover and microwave on high (100 percent) power for 8 minutes. Stir the mixture twice during cooking.

Meanwhile, for the dumplings, sift the remaining 1¼ cups flour with the baking powder and ¼ teaspoon of the salt. Stir in the parsley and milk until just blended.

Remove the chicken mixture from the microwave and stir in the peas, the remaining ¼ teaspoon salt, and the pepper. With a spoon, mold 6 dumplings from the flour mixture and spoon them over the chicken.

Microwave on high, uncovered, for 6 to 7 minutes, until a toothpick inserted into a dumpling comes out clean. Remove the bay leaf and serve hot.

NUTRITIONAL CONTENT PER SERVING: **Calories: 304   Protein: 25 g Carbohydrates: 29 g   Fat: 9 g   Saturated fat: 2 g   Cholesterol: 64 mg Sodium: 396 mg   Fiber: 2 g   27 percent calories from fat**

Tex-Mex Chicken Pockets

Firefighter Anthony "The Gooch" Catera

Serves 6

Engine Company 273

New York City Fire Department

Flushing, New York

This is a spicy sandwich that can be cooked in a flash as long as the pan is hot enough for stir-frying. Pita bread is very low in fat and makes a handy pocket for cooked fillings like this one.

1½ pounds skinless, boneless chicken breasts, cut in 1-inch pieces
2 tablespoons olive oil, divided
1 teaspoon chili powder
½ teaspoon ground cumin
½ teaspoon dried oregano
1 clove garlic, finely chopped
2 scallions, chopped
One 4-ounce can chopped green chiles
1 small jalapeño pepper, seeded and finely chopped
One 15-ounce can black beans, drained and rinsed
6 whole wheat pita breads
1 head iceberg lettuce, shredded
¾ cup prepared salsa

In a medium bowl, toss the chicken pieces with 1 tablespoon of the olive oil and the chili powder, cumin, and oregano.

Heat a large nonstick skillet over medium-high heat. When it is hot, add the remaining 1 tablespoon of olive oil and swirl to coat the inside of the skillet.

Add the seasoned chicken and stir-fry for about 4 minutes, until it is barely cooked through.

Add the garlic, scallions, chiles, and jalapeño pepper. Stir-fry for about 1 minute, until the scallions soften. Stir in the beans and cook for about 2 minutes, until they are heated through.

Slice a small opening in one end of each pita. Fill each with some of the shredded lettuce, the stir-fried mixture, and the salsa. Serve hot.

NUTRITIONAL CONTENT PER SERVING: Calories: 427   Protein: 35 g
Carbohydrates: 53 g   Fat: 9 g   Saturated fat: 2 g   Cholesterol: 58 mg
Sodium: 820 mg   Fiber: 9 g   29 percent calories from fat

Chicken Interdonati

Firefighter James "Buff" Interdonati   Serves 4
Ladder Company 129
New York City Fire Department
Flushing, New York

Although Jim is a firefighter, his nickname, Buff, means someone who loves firefighting and anything and everything to do with it. There are lots of buffs out there, I suppose because there is something romantic and alluring that the general public attaches to firefighting—I have literally seen it on the faces of passersby as we ride to an alarm. Jim is also a fire marshal for the Port Washington Volunteer Fire Department on Long Island, a job he performs in his spare time. We call him Buff because he loves his jobs (paid and volunteer) so much. This is one of his favorite Italian dishes.

continued

2¾ pounds chicken thighs (about 8 thighs), skinned
1½ teaspoons Italian herb seasoning
½ teaspoon black pepper
1 medium onion, sliced
2 large cloves garlic, finely chopped
Two 16-ounce cans stewed tomatoes, undrained
½ cup dry white wine
One 12-ounce package yolk-free egg noodles

Sprinkle the chicken liberally with the Italian herb seasoning and the pepper.

In a large nonstick Dutch oven, cook the chicken over medium heat for about 10 minutes, until browned on both sides. Turn the chicken several times during cooking to ensure even browning. Remove the chicken from the pot, transfer to a plate, and set aside.

Add the onion and garlic to the Dutch oven and cook for about 5 minutes, until lightly browned. Add the stewed tomatoes and wine. Return the chicken to the pot and bring it to a boil. Reduce the heat to low and simmer for 30 minutes, stirring occasionally, until the chicken shows no sign of pink when cut at the bone.

Cook the noodles according to package directions. Spoon the sauce and chicken over the noodles and serve immediately.

NUTRITIONAL CONTENT PER SERVING: **Calories: 374   Protein: 32 g**
Carbohydrates: 46 g   Fat: 10 g   Saturated fat: 2 g   Cholesterol: 63 mg
Sodium: 333 mg   Fiber: 6 g   24 percent calories from fat

The Healthy Firehouse Cookbook

Balsamic Chicken Simmer

Serves 6

2¾ pounds skinless, boneless chicken thighs
¼ teaspoon salt
⅛ teaspoon black pepper
2 tablespoons chopped shallots
2 tablespoons balsamic vinegar

Spray a large nonstick skillet with nonstick cooking spray and heat over medium-high heat. Season the chicken with the salt and pepper. Cook for about 6 minutes, turning frequently, until the chicken is browned on all sides. Cover, reduce the heat to medium, and cook for about 10 minutes, until the juices run clear when the chicken is pierced with a knife.

Add the shallots and cook for about 1 minute, until they soften. Stir in the balsamic vinegar and cook for 30 seconds, turning the chicken to coat thoroughly. Serve immediately.

NUTRITIONAL CONTENT PER SERVING: **Calories: 139   Protein: 20 g
Carbohydrates: 1 g   Fat: 5 g   Saturated fat: 1 g   Cholesterol: 61 mg
Sodium: 106 mg   Fiber: 0 g   36 percent calories from fat**

Turkey Lasagna

For bodybuilders to maintain lean muscle, they should eat a diet composed of 30 percent protein, 60 percent carbohydrates, and 10 percent fat. Of course, not everyone is into bodybuilding, and the guidelines from the American Heart Association allow 25 to 30 percent fat per day—but it never hurts to have a recipe on hand that contributes a large amount of protein and carbohydrates and relatively little fat, as with this lasagna. Its proportions of protein, carbohydrates, and fat are just about on target for bodybuilding. Heed the warning about washing your hands and work surfaces with warm soap and water, which is given in the recipe note for Spinach Turkey Roll on page 194.

1 pound ground turkey
1 small onion, chopped
4 cups prepared spaghetti sauce
12 lasagna noodles
1 cup nonfat ricotta cheese
6 ounces part-skim mozzarella cheese, shredded (about 1½ cups)
2 tablespoons grated Parmesan cheese

Preheat the oven to 350°F.

Spray the inside of a large nonstick skillet with nonstick cooking spray. Add the ground turkey and onion and cook for 5 to 7 minutes, until the meat loses its pink color, stirring often to break up the turkey.

Drain off the fat and stir in the spaghetti sauce. Cook over low heat for 15 minutes.

Meanwhile, bring a large pot of lightly salted water to a boil, add the lasagna noodles, and cook for about 10 minutes, until the noodles are just tender. Drain, rinse under cold water, and drain again.

Spray a 13-by-9-inch baking pan with nonstick cooking spray and arrange 4 lasagna noodles in the bottom. Top with a third of the meat sauce, half of the ricotta cheese, and half of the mozzarella cheese. Arrange 4 more lasagna noodles on top of the cheese and top with half of the remaining sauce and the rest of the ricotta and mozzarella cheeses. Arrange the last 4 noodles on top of the cheese and spread with the remaining sauce.

Sprinkle the Parmesan cheese on top of the lasagna. Bake for about 35 minutes, until the lasagna is hot and bubbling. Let stand for 10 minutes before serving.

NUTRITIONAL CONTENT PER SERVING: Calories: 427   Protein: 30 g
Carbohydrates: 56 g   Fat: 10 g   Saturated fat: 4 g   Cholesterol: 44 mg
Sodium: 604 mg   Fiber: 4 g   21 percent calories from fat

Chicken Laterza

Firefighter Joseph Laterza

Serves 6

Ladder Company 129

New York City Fire Department

Flushing, New York

This became a firehouse favorite because the chicken could stand in the broth and mushrooms in the refrigerator if we were called to an alarm. The longer it stayed in the broth, the more tender and juicy it became. It's never a good idea to leave uncooked or cooked chicken at room temperature for any length of time, so if you plan to delay serving this meal, refrigerate it after it has cooked and then warm it up on top of the stove or in the oven.

3½ cups chicken broth, preferably homemade (page 110), or canned
  low-sodium broth
1 cup dry cooking sherry
8 ounces fresh mushrooms, quartered
½ cup liquid egg substitute or 4 egg whites
1½ cups dried seasoned bread crumbs
Six 5-ounce skinless, boneless chicken breast halves, cut in half
Two 16-ounce packages yolk-free egg noodles
1 tablespoon cornstarch
½ cup cold water

Preheat the oven to 350°F.

In a 13-by-9-inch baking dish, combine the chicken broth, sherry, and mushrooms. Bake for about 20 minutes, until the mushrooms soften.

Meanwhile, pour the liquid egg substitute into a shallow dish and spread the bread crumbs on a plate. Dip the chicken pieces into the egg and then into the crumbs. Pat to help the crumbs adhere to the chicken.

Spray a nonstick skillet with nonstick cooking spray and heat over medium heat. In as many batches as necessary, cook the chicken for about 5 minutes, turning once or twice to ensure even browning. Remove the chicken from the skillet and set aside.

When the mushrooms have softened, add the browned chicken to the baking pan and return it to the oven. Bake for about 15 minutes, until the chicken is cooked through.

Meanwhile, bring a large pot of lightly salted water to a boil, add the noodles, and cook for about 9 minutes, until tender. Drain well.

In a small bowl, whisk the cornstarch and water until the cornstarch is dissolved. Stir the mixture into the baking dish and bake for about 3 minutes, until the sauce has thickened.

Spoon the chicken and sauce over the noodles and serve immediately.

NUTRITIONAL CONTENT PER SERVING: **Calories: 519   Protein: 44 g**
Carbohydrates: 56 g   Fat: 6 g   Saturated fat: 1 g   Cholesterol: 70 mg
Sodium: 157 mg   Fiber: 4 g   11 percent calories from fat

Home on LaGrange Grilled Turkey

Firefighter Robert A. LaGrange
Winton Fire Department
Winton, Iowa

Serves 8

If you like the flavors of Southeast Asia, you will appreciate this peanutty grilled turkey. Robert LaGrange sent me this recipe from Iowa, and as soon as I tried it, I loved it. It's great to make in the summer, when the charcoal grill is in constant operation. The turkey is placed over a pan that is positioned next to the coals to catch the drippings during cooking. This prevents flareups and allows the meat to be cooked by indirect heat, and so it is moister than you might expect. If you don't have a charcoal grill, bake the turkey in a 400°F oven for 1 hour.

⅓ cup unsalted peanut butter
⅓ cup teriyaki sauce
¼ cup apricot jam
¼ cup fresh lemon juice
1 tablespoon grated fresh ginger or 2 teaspoons ground ginger
2 teaspoons dried basil
2 scallions, coarsely chopped
2 cloves garlic, finely chopped
½ teaspoon crushed hot red pepper flakes
Two 1½-pound skinless, boneless turkey breast halves

Combine the peanut butter, teriyaki sauce, apricot jam, lemon juice, ginger, basil, scallions, garlic, and red pepper flakes in a blender or food processor and process until smooth.

Lay the turkey breasts in a shallow nonaluminum dish and spread the peanut butter mixture on top. Cover and refrigerate for at least 1 hour and up to 4 hours. Turn occasionally.

Lightly oil the grill rack of a covered charcoal grill. On one side of the grill, build a hot fire. On the empty side, set a shallow heatproof pan. Put the grill rack in place.

Remove the turkey breasts from the marinade, reserving the marinade. Place the turkey on the grill rack over the pan and slather it well with the reserved marinade. Cover and grill with all vents open for 50 minutes to 1 hour, until a meat thermometer inserted in the thickest part of the turkey reads 165°F.

Let stand for 5 minutes, then cut crosswise in diagonal slices and serve.

NUTRITIONAL CONTENT PER SERVING: **Calories: 197 Protein: 24 g
Carbohydrates: 13 g   Fat: 6 g   Saturated fat: 1 g   Cholesterol: 58 mg
Sodium: 499 mg   Fiber: 1 g   26 percent calories from fat**

Rockaway Jambalaya

Firefighter Bob Redman

Engine Company 265

New York City Fire Department

Rockaway Beach, New York

Serves 6

One of the challenges of compiling the recipes for this book was getting them in workable form. Many great firehouse cooks never write down their recipes and, when asked to do so, provide "exact" measurements such as "a little of this" and "a whole bunch of that." When I worked a day tour with Bob, he cooked this great jambalaya for lunch, and between alarms and cooking we were able to get the ingredients down on paper.

½ pound hot or sweet Italian sausage, pierced with a fork

½ cup water

1 pound skinless, boneless chicken breasts, cut in 1-inch cubes

4 cups chicken broth, preferably homemade (page 110), or canned
   low-sodium broth

1½ cups long-grain white rice

½ cup chopped fresh parsley

1 small onion, chopped

½ cup chopped scallions

1 small green bell pepper, seeded and finely chopped

¼ cup tomato paste

2 teaspoons Cajun spice seasoning

¼ teaspoon cayenne pepper

¼ teaspoon black pepper

Spray a large nonstick skillet with nonstick cooking spray and heat over medium heat. Add the sausage and water and cook for about 12 minutes, until the water is evaporated and the sausage is well browned. Remove the sausage from the skillet and slice ½ inch thick. Transfer the sausage slices to a large Dutch oven.

Wash the skillet and spray it again with nonstick cooking spray. Add the chicken to the skillet and cook over medium heat for about 6 minutes, turning occasionally to ensure that it browns evenly. Transfer the chicken to the Dutch oven.

Stir in the chicken broth, rice, parsley, onion, scallions, green pepper, tomato paste, Cajun seasoning, cayenne, and black pepper. Bring to a boil, reduce the heat to low, and simmer, covered, for about 20 minutes, until the rice is tender. Let stand for 5 minutes before serving.

NUTRITIONAL CONTENT PER SERVING: **Calories: 354 Protein: 26 g Carbohydrates: 40 g Fat: 9 g Saturated fat: 3 g Cholesterol: 56 mg Sodium: 765 mg Fiber 1 g 23 percent calories from fat**

Bigfoot's Motor Home Skillet Chicken

Firefighter Gary "Bigfoot" Marozas
Engine Company 273
New York City Fire Department
Flushing, New York

Serves 8

Gary is 6 feet 7 inches tall, weighs 300 pounds, and wears size 15 shoes. He earned his nickname for obvious reasons! When vacation rolls around, Gary gets in his beat-up motor home, which we have dubbed "the rolling tenement," and travels around the United States. He was a star basketball player for St. John's University and now is working on getting back into shape. Recipes like this hearty one-dish meal are helping him—he makes it on the small stove in the motor home and, if we're lucky, at the firehouse.

One 12-ounce package yolk-free egg noodles
2 tablespoons canola or other vegetable oil, divided
10 ounces skinless, boneless chicken breast, cut into 1-by-2-inch strips
1 small onion, halved and thinly sliced
1 large carrot, sliced diagonally ¼ inch thick
1 red bell pepper, seeded and sliced ½ inch thick
1 clove garlic, finely chopped
¼ cup fresh lemon juice
¼ cup water
1 tablespoon Worcestershire sauce
2 teaspoons cornstarch
½ teaspoon salt
¼ teaspoon black pepper
Chopped fresh parsley

Bring a large pot of lightly salted water to a boil, add the noodles, and cook for about 8 minutes, until they are just tender. Drain, rinse under cold water, and drain again. Set aside.

In a large nonstick skillet, heat 1 tablespoon of the oil over medium heat. Cook the chicken for about 6 minutes, stirring occasionally to ensure even browning. Transfer the chicken to a plate and set aside.

Heat the remaining oil in the skillet and add the onion, carrot, red pepper, and garlic. Cook for about 5 minutes, stirring constantly, until the vegetables are crisp-tender.

In a small bowl, whisk the lemon juice, water, Worcestershire sauce, cornstarch, salt, and pepper until the cornstarch is dissolved. Add the cooked noodles and chicken to the skillet and stir in the cornstarch mixture. Bring to a simmer and cook for about 1 minute, until the sauce thickens. Sprinkle with parsley and serve hot.

NUTRITIONAL CONTENT PER SERVING: **Calories: 278   Protein: 20 g Carbohydrates: 36 g   Fat: 5 g   Saturated fat: 2 g   Cholesterol: 37 mg Sodium: 498 mg   Fiber: 3 g   16 percent calories from fat**

Chicken in a Cockloft

Firefighter Rick Margino

Serves 8

Ladder Company 129

New York City Fire Department

Flushing, New York

In this recipe the chicken is baked in a pan covered with a "lid" of aluminum foil, and so we firefighters call it "Chicken in a Cockloft." A cockloft is the area between the ceiling of the attic (or top floor) and the actual roof. It often is an unused space where there is a lot of old wood. Needless to say, it is susceptible to an accelerating fire, and firefighters are wisely wary of entering the cockloft of any building. My fellow firefighter Rick Margino developed this recipe, which has become a great favorite in our firehouse. Rick is always interested in healthy eating and keeping physically fit. He and I not only cook together; we also work out together in the basement of the firehouse.

2 tablespoons olive oil

1 large onion, sliced

1½ pounds fresh mushrooms, sliced

3 cloves garlic, minced

2 cups dry white cooking wine

1 cup chicken broth, preferably homemade (page 110), or canned
   low-sodium broth

2 tablespoons chopped fresh parsley

1 teaspoon dried tarragon

¼ teaspoon black pepper

½ cup liquid egg substitute or 4 large egg whites

¾ cup dried seasoned bread crumbs

2 pounds skinless, boneless chicken breasts, cut in 1-inch pieces

3 ripe medium tomatoes, cut in 8 wedges

1 large red bell pepper, seeded and sliced ½ inch thick

1 pound tricolor rotini

In a large nonstick skillet, heat the oil. Add the onion and cook for about 3 minutes, until it softens. Add the mushrooms and garlic and cook for about 3 minutes, stirring often, until the mushrooms are lightly browned.

Stir in the wine, chicken broth, parsley, tarragon, and black pepper. Reduce the heat to low and simmer for 20 minutes.

Preheat the oven to 350°F. Pour the egg substitute into a medium bowl and spread the bread crumbs on a shallow plate. Dip the chicken pieces into the egg substitute and then into the bread crumbs. Pat to help the crumbs adhere to the chicken.

Transfer the chicken to a 13-by-9-inch baking dish. Pour the mushroom mixture over the chicken and then top with the tomatoes and bell pepper strips. Cover tightly with aluminum foil. Bake for about 30 minutes, until hot and bubbling.

Meanwhile, bring a pot of lightly salted water to a boil, add the pasta, and cook for about 9 minutes, until al dente. Drain well.

Spoon the chicken, vegetables, and sauce over the hot pasta and serve immediately.

NUTRITIONAL CONTENT PER SERVING: **Calories: 290   Protein: 38 g**

Carbohydrates: 13 g   Fat: 5 g   Saturated fat: 1 g   Cholesterol: 90 mg

Sodium: 175 mg   Fiber: 2 g   16 percent calories from fat

Asian Foil-Wrapped Chicken

Firefighter Jennifer Perley

Madbury Volunteer Fire Department

Madbury, New Hampshire

Serves 4

They say good things come in small packages, and these foil-wrapped chicken breasts are absolutely wonderful to serve at home or at the firehouse. The recipe was contributed by a firefighter from New Hampshire who volunteers for a small department with 28 members. In contrast, New York City has approximately 8,500 active firefighters on duty. But we appreciate the good things in Jennifer's small foil packets.

3 tablespoons low-sodium soy sauce

1 tablespoon Asian sesame oil

½ teaspoon grated fresh ginger

1 clove garlic, minced

Four 5-ounce skinless, boneless chicken breast halves

1 large red bell pepper, seeded and sliced ½ inch thick

¼ pound snow peas

½ cup sliced water chestnuts

2 scallions, chopped

2 cups hot cooked rice

Preheat the oven to 500°F. Spray four 12-inch-square sheets of aluminum foil with nonstick cooking spray.

In a small bowl, mix the soy sauce, oil, ginger, and garlic.

Place the foil squares, oiled side up, on a work surface. Lay a chicken cutlet in the bottom half of each foil square and fold the edges up but not over the chicken. Scatter the red pepper strips, snow peas, water chestnuts, and scallions evenly over the 4 chicken breasts. Spoon equal amounts of the soy sauce mixture over the vegetables.

Fold the foil over the chicken and roll up the edges tightly to seal. Place the foil packets on a baking sheet.

Bake for 12 minutes. Check for doneness by opening one of the foil packets to see if the chicken is firm and the juices run clear when the meat is pierced with a knife.

To serve, place each foil packet on a dinner plate. Allow each guest to cut open his or her own packet and spoon rice over the chicken.

NUTRITIONAL CONTENT PER SERVING: **Calories: 217   Protein: 29 g**

Carbohydrates: 9 g   Fat: 7 g   Saturated fat: 1 g   Cholesterol: 73 mg

Sodium: 839 mg   Fiber: 2 g   29 percent calories from fat

The Christmas Turkey

Fires don't take holidays and consequently neither do firefighters. We love our jobs, but even so, we would rather be home on Christmas Eve than in the firehouse. I remember the Christmas Eve of 1982 when I was assigned the night tour. At that time I was with an engine company in Queens, working with a lieutenant nicknamed Wolf, who was well known in the department as a great guy and a great firefighter. Wolf and I decided to make the best of the situation and began preparing a real holiday meal: roast turkey, mashed potatoes, stuffing, green beans, and so on. At 9:30, just after we had put our beautifully dressed turkey in the oven, the alarm sounded. We expected it to be a false alarm or small incident (wishful holiday thinking!), and so, when we left, we only turned off the stove burners. The turkey, we reasoned, would be just about done when we returned.

Smoke was pouring from the casement windows of the building when we pulled up minutes later. We were first on the scene and no ladder company was in sight. I grabbed a forcible entry tool called a halligan and pried open a window. With a boost from me, Wolf hoisted himself in and then pulled me in along with a 2½-gallon water extinguisher. We crawled on our knees through the smoke-filled living room and found an elderly man, his clothes in flames, in the rear of the room. The room was beginning to light up (tongues of fire were starting to lash out in addition to the smoke-producing smoldering fire). I doused the man with water and we dragged him to the door just as the ladder company was breaking through it. The man survived and the fire was easily contained, but the entire episode, which included a good deal of paperwork, took far longer than we had anticipated. Toward the end of the evening, Wolf and I looked at each other and, figuratively slapping our foreheads, exclaimed in unison: "The turkey!"

A thoroughly burned turkey and a good measure of exhaustion resulted in a Christmas meal of peanut butter and jelly sandwiches. But we had saved a life. The chief recommended Wolf for a citation, but being a humble man, he insisted the citation go to the entire company. No firefighter could ask for a better Christmas present.

Turkey Bob with Lime and Honey

Firefighter Jennifer Perley
Madbury Volunteer Fire Department
Madbury, New Hampshire

Serves 6

Turkey has much less fat than other meats, and so it will dry out when it is grilled if your fire is too hot. Use medium-hot coals and test the fire's temperature: Hold your hand about six inches over the coals and start counting. If you can only reach one or two, your fire is very hot, fine for beef steaks or hamburgers but not for turkey. When you can count to three, the coals are medium-hot, perfect for poultry. Be sure to use a grill with a lid to capture the heat. If you don't have such a grill, fashion a temporary lid out of a tent of crumpled heavy-duty foil. These turkey kabobs are threaded on bamboo skewers and are easy to buy in any grocery store. Be sure to soak them before using so that they won't ignite during cooking. You can, of course, use metal skewers.

¼ cup fresh lime juice
¼ cup honey
3 tablespoons dried oregano
2 tablespoons canola or other vegetable oil
2 cloves garlic, minced
½ teaspoon salt
½ teaspoon cayenne pepper
½ teaspoon black pepper
3 pounds turkey breast medallions, cut in 1-inch cubes
2 red onions, quartered
2 green bell peppers, quartered and seeded
2 red bell peppers, quartered and seeded

continued

In a large glass bowl, combine the lime juice, honey, oregano, oil, garlic, salt, cayenne, and black pepper to make a marinade. Add the turkey cubes, onions, and bell peppers and toss well. Cover and refrigerate for at least 1 hour or up to 4 hours.

Soak 6 bamboo skewers in water for 30 minutes.

Build a medium-hot fire in a charcoal grill and lightly oil the grill rack, or preheat a gas grill to medium heat, or preheat the broiler. Drain the bamboo skewers.

Drain and discard the marinade from the turkey and vegetables. Thread the turkey and vegetables onto the soaked bamboo skewers, alternating the turkey with the onions and red and green peppers.

Set the kabobs on the grill, lower the cover, and grill for 10 to 12 minutes, until the juices run clear when the turkey is pierced with a sharp knife. If you're using a broiler, broil for 10 to 12 minutes, until the juices run clear.

NUTRITIONAL CONTENT PER SERVING: Calories: 233   Protein: 31 g
Carbohydrates: 11 g   Fat: 7 g   Saturated fat: 2 g   Cholesterol: 77 mg
Sodium: 74 mg   Fiber: 1 g   27 percent calories from fat

Rick's Sizzlin' Skillet Chicken

Firefighter Richard Duden   Serves 4
Ladder Company 129
New York City Fire Department
Flushing, New York

This recipe is fast, easy, and low in fat—what could be better? We call it "sizzlin' " because the chicken cooks in a hot skillet, getting nice and brown.

Four 5-ounce skinless, boneless chicken breast halves, sliced thin

¼ teaspoon salt

⅛ teaspoon black pepper

1 onion, chopped

1 green bell pepper, seeded and sliced ½ inch thick

2 cloves garlic, minced

2 cups crushed tomatoes

1 teaspoon dried basil

½ teaspoon dried oregano

2 tablespoons chopped fresh basil or parsley

Spray a large nonstick skillet with nonstick cooking spray and heat over medium heat. Season the chicken breasts with salt and pepper. Cook the chicken for about 4 minutes, turning to ensure even browning on all sides. Remove from the skillet and set aside, covered, to keep warm.

Add the onion and green pepper to the skillet. Cover and cook over medium heat for about 5 minutes, until the onion softens. Add the garlic and stir for 1 minute. Stir in the crushed tomatoes, basil, and oregano. Bring to a simmer, reduce the heat to low, and cook for 10 minutes.

Return the chicken to the skillet and cook for about 10 minutes, until the juices run clear when the chicken is pierced with a sharp knife. Serve immediately, sprinkled with the fresh basil or parsley.

NUTRITIONAL CONTENT PER SERVING: **Calories: 349   Protein: 36 g**
Carbohydrates: 35 g   Fat: 7 g   Saturated fat: 2 g   Cholesterol: 87 mg
Sodium: 87 mg   Fiber: 2 g   17 percent calories from fat

"All Hands" Meat Loaf

Although you usually think of making meat loaf with beef, pork, or both, this loaf is made with ground turkey, which is far lower in fat and calories. Setting the loaf on a rack raised above the roasting pan allows what little fat there is to drain off during cooking. "All hands" is the radio signal given by the officer to alert firefighters that there is a working fire in progress. This dish will definitely bring "all hands" to the table.

2 pounds ground turkey
1 onion, finely chopped
2 stalks celery, finely chopped
1 cup rolled oats
1 cup tomato sauce, divided
⅔ cup skim milk
½ cup oat bran
¼ cup liquid egg substitute or 2 egg whites, lightly beaten
2 teaspoons minced fresh parsley
1 teaspoon dried rosemary
1 teaspoon dried tarragon
1 teaspoon dried thyme
1 teaspoon salt
½ teaspoon black pepper
¼ teaspoon hot red pepper sauce

Preheat the oven to 350°F. Place a large piece of aluminum foil on a roasting rack and pierce the foil all over with the tip of a knife.

In a large bowl, combine all the ingredients except 2 tablespoons of the tomato sauce. Mix thoroughly by hand. Place the mixture on top of the foil-lined rack and form a 10-by-5-inch loaf.

With the back of a spoon, make a shallow valley down the length of the loaf and fill it with the remaining 2 tablespoons of tomato sauce.

Bake for 1 to 1¼ hours, until a meat thermometer inserted in the center of the loaf reads 165°F.

NUTRITIONAL CONTENT PER SERVING: Calories: 176   Protein: 25 g
Carbohydrates: 16 g   Fat: 2 g   Saturated fat: 1 g   Cholesterol: 59 mg
Sodium: 266 mg   Fiber: 3 g   10 percent calories from fat

Chopped Meat?

I was working overtime once in a ladder company in Queens and offered to help prepare the evening meal. The crew was making meat loaf, and when I commented on the especially large quantity of chopped meat, I was told they always saved a little for their pets. I had worked in enough firehouses to know I might be setting myself open for a practical joke if I pursued my questioning, and so I simply sat back, peeled potatoes, and watched. One of the firefighters fashioned about two pounds of meat into a "man" with arms, legs, head, and torso and cooked his creation in a huge cast-iron skillet. It was then set aside while we sat down to our meal. Just as the meal ended, we were called out on an alarm involving an automobile accident. When we got back to the firehouse, I was invited to watch the firefighters feed their pets. We marched to a back room where the meat loaf man was waved in front of a large tank holding three hungry piranhas—flesh-eating fish from South America. The taunting riled the fish, and when the meat was dropped into the tank, it was devoured in about thirty seconds.

O'Neill's Honey-Mustard Pork

Firefighter Kevin O'Neill   Serves 6

Ladder Company 129

New York City Fire Department

Flushing, New York

Kevin recently transferred from Ladder Company 46 in the Bronx to our company and brought with him a special talent: He's an excellent cook. Cooking is not his only talent. He also appeared in the A&E film *FDNY, Brothers in Battle.* If the butcher does not have pork loin steaks for this amazingly fast and easy recipe, ask him to cut them from a boneless pork loin roast.

½ cup honey
½ cup Dijon-style mustard
2 cups dried seasoned bread crumbs
Six 8-ounce boneless pork loin steaks, about 1 inch thick, well trimmed

Preheat the oven to 350°F.

In a medium bowl, whisk together the honey and mustard until smooth. Spread the bread crumbs on a plate.

Dip each pork loin steak first into the honey-mustard mixture and then into the bread crumbs. Pat to help the crumbs adhere to the meat.

Set a roasting rack in a roasting pan. Stand each steak vertically between the slats of the rack. Bake for about 30 minutes, until the juices run clear when pierced with a sharp knife. Serve hot.

NUTRITIONAL CONTENT PER SERVING: **Calories: 464   Protein: 33 g   Carbohydrates: 49 g   Fat: 15 g   Saturated fat: 5 g   Cholesterol: 91 mg   Sodium: 571 mg   Fiber: 1 g   29 percent calories from fat**

Fruit-Stuffed Pork Tenderloin

Firefighter Jennifer Perley

Madbury Volunteer Fire Department

Madbury, New Hampshire

Serves 4

Here's another recipe from our friend in New Hampshire. Although the Madbury Fire Department is small, they obviously eat well! I have tried to keep the percentage of calories from fat below 30 percent in every recipe in this book, but this one is one of the exceptions to the rule. It's a little higher but worth every bite. And after all, every once in a while it's okay to indulge a little.

¼ cup dried currants
¼ cup dried apricots, finely chopped
2 tablespoons bourbon
1 tablespoon water
1 cup fresh pumpernickel bread crumbs
2 egg whites
¼ teaspoon dried rosemary
⅛ teaspoon dried sage
¼ teaspoon salt
⅛ teaspoon black pepper
1 pound boneless pork tenderloin

Preheat the oven to 400°F. In a medium bowl, soak the currants and apricots in the bourbon and water for at least 30 minutes.

Stir the bread crumbs, egg whites, rosemary, sage, salt, and pepper into the fruit and mix well.

Using a sharp knife, make a deep incision down the length of the tenderloin, being careful not to cut all the way through. Spread the tenderloin open and lay it between 2 sheets of moistened waxed paper. With a meat mallet, pound the tenderloin until it flattens to ¼ inch in thickness. Spread the fruit mixture over the meat, leaving a 1-inch border. Roll the meat lengthwise and tie it closed with kitchen string. Place on a rack in a roasting pan.

Bake for 40 to 50 minutes, until a meat thermometer inserted in the center of the tenderloin reads 155°F. Remove from the oven and let stand for 5 minutes, then remove the string and slice to serve.

NUTRITIONAL CONTENT PER SERVING: **Calories: 293   Protein: 26 g**
Carbohydrates: 18 g   Fat: 11 g   Saturated fat: 4 g   Cholesterol: 125 mg
Sodium: 266 mg   Fiber: 2 g   37 percent calories from fat

Dumpster Beef Stroganoff

Firefighter Gary Dempsey
Engine Company 273
New York City Fire Department
Flushing, New York

Serves 6

Beef stroganoff is a dish most people associate with all the "bad" things—those foods we're told over and over *not* to eat. But with Gary's version, you can have your stroganoff and lean body too! The recipe calls for very lean beef and nonfat sour cream substitute, which is good when used this way. Why do we call it "dumpster" stroganoff? The irony is that this never ends up in the garbage—it's much too popular in the firehouse.

1 pound beef tenderloin, fat trimmed, cut into ½-by-2-inch strips
¼ teaspoon salt
¼ teaspoon black pepper
½ pound fresh mushrooms, sliced
1 medium onion, finely chopped
2 cloves garlic, finely chopped
1⅓ cups beef broth, preferably homemade (page 112), or canned
    low-sodium broth
1 teaspoon dried tarragon
One 16-ounce package yolk-free egg noodles
1 cup nonfat sour cream substitute
1 tablespoon finely chopped fresh dill

Spray a large nonstick skillet with nonstick cooking spray and heat over medium-high heat. Season the beef with the salt and pepper. In as many batches as necessary, cook the beef strips for about 5 minutes, turning occasionally, until they are browned on all sides. Transfer the beef to a plate and cover with foil to keep warm.

Add the mushrooms, onion, and garlic to the skillet; cover and cook over medium heat for about 5 minutes, until the mushrooms soften. Stir in the beef broth and the tarragon. Bring to a boil, reduce the heat to low, and simmer, partially covered, for 15 minutes. Then return the beef strips to the skillet.

Meanwhile, bring a large pot of lightly salted water to a boil, add the noodles, and cook for about 9 minutes, until they are tender. Drain well and set aside.

Stir the sour cream substitute into the skillet and cook just until heated through; do not boil once the cream has been added. Spoon the stroganoff over the noodles, sprinkle with the dill, and serve immediately.

NUTRITIONAL CONTENT PER SERVING: **Calories: 347   Protein: 27 g
Carbohydrates: 48 g   Fat: 5 g   Saturated fat: 2 g   Cholesterol: 40 mg
Sodium: 251 mg   Fiber: 4 g   13 percent calories from fat**

Oriental Brown Rice and Beef Hash

Firefighter Billy Whetzel
Rescue 2
Washington, D.C., Fire Department
Washington, D.C.

Serves 4

Hash used to be what you'd get on a blue plate special in diners. Usually it was made of chopped-up leftover meat mixed with cubed potatoes and onions and then cooked almost to death. This recipe is a thoroughly modern version—no potatoes, no leftovers, and no overcooking. Instead, it has a slightly Asian flavor and is made with spinach, tomatoes, and nutrient-rich brown rice.

1 tablespoon canola or other vegetable oil
1 small onion, finely chopped
1 small green bell pepper, seeded and finely chopped
1 clove garlic, finely chopped
2 teaspoons grated fresh ginger
1 pound extra-lean ground sirloin
4 cups cooked brown rice
4 ounces fresh spinach, well rinsed, stems removed, and cut into ½-inch
    strips
2 plum tomatoes, cut into ½-inch cubes
2 tablespoons low-sodium soy sauce
⅛ teaspoon black pepper

In a large nonstick skillet, heat the oil over medium-high heat. Add the onion, green pepper, garlic, and ginger and stir-fry for about 2 minutes, until the vegetables soften. Add the ground sirloin and cook for about 5 minutes, until the meat loses its pink color, stirring often to break up the beef.

Stir in the cooked brown rice, spinach, tomatoes, soy sauce, and black pepper. Cook for about 3 minutes, stirring often, until the spinach is wilted and the rice is heated through. Serve immediately.

NUTRITIONAL CONTENT PER SERVING: **Calories: 287   Protein: 18 g
Carbohydrates: 33 g   Fat: 9 g   Saturated fat: 2 g   Cholesterol: 44 mg
Sodium: 728 mg   Fiber: 3 g   28 percent calories from fat**

Shepherd's Pie × 12

Firefighter Anita Livesey
Engine Company 10
Washington, D.C., Fire Department
Washington, D.C.

Serves 12

This is a meal to feed a bunch of hungry firefighters if ever there was one, and yet it's quite low in fat because it's made with nonfat sour cream and low-fat Cheddar. It's good to remember that it's not the potatoes spread on top of classic shepherd's pie that adds the calories and fat but what is mixed into them (ingredients such as butter and cream).

8 large baking potatoes (about 6 pounds), peeled and cut into large cubes
2 tablespoons canola or other vegetable oil
5 pounds extra-lean ground sirloin
2 large onions, chopped
2 green bell peppers, seeded and chopped
2 stalks celery, chopped
One 16-ounce can tomato sauce
¼ cup low-sodium Worcestershire sauce
1 teaspoon salt, divided
¼ teaspoon black pepper
One 8-ounce container nonfat sour cream substitute
8 ounces low-fat Cheddar cheese, shredded (about 2 cups)
4 large egg whites
½ cup freshly grated Parmesan cheese

Preheat the oven to 375°F.

Bring a large pot of lightly salted water to a boil, add the potatoes, and cook for about 20 minutes, until tender. Drain well.

Meanwhile, in a Dutch oven, heat the oil over medium-high heat. Add the ground sirloin, onions, peppers, and celery and cook for about 10 minutes, until the meat loses its pink color, stirring often to break up the beef. Drain off any excess fat.

Stir in the tomato sauce, Worcestershire sauce, ½ teaspoon of the salt, and the pepper. Ladle equal amounts of the mixture into two 13-by-9-inch casserole dishes.

Transfer the drained potatoes to a large mixing bowl and mash them with the sour cream substitute, Cheddar cheese, egg whites, and remaining salt. Spread half of the mashed potatoes on top of each casserole. Sprinkle each with Parmesan cheese. Bake for 30 to 40 minutes, until golden brown. Serve hot.

NUTRITIONAL CONTENT PER SERVING: **Calories: 675   Protein: 52 g**
Carbohydrates: 72 g   Fat: 19 g   Saturated fat: 7 g   Cholesterol: 161 mg
Sodium: 705 mg   Fiber: 7 g   20 percent calories from fat

Fire Bell Stuffed Peppers

Lieutenant Fred Schlueck
Engine Company 313
New York City Fire Department
Douglaston, New York

Serves 4

These simple stuffed bell peppers are quite low in fat and calories because they call for lean ground sirloin. Look for chopped meat that is 90 percent lean. The brown rice provides good nutrients and necessary fiber.

½ cup brown rice
½ pound lean ground sirloin
1 small onion, finely chopped
½ teaspoon dried marjoram
¼ teaspoon salt
⅛ teaspoon black pepper
4 green bell peppers, tops cut off and seeds removed
One 10¾-ounce can low-sodium tomato soup
¾ cup water

Bring a large saucepan of lightly salted water a boil, add the rice, and cook for about 50 minutes, until it is barely tender. Drain well.

Preheat the oven to 350°F. Lightly spray the inside of an 11-by-7-inch baking dish with nonstick cooking spray.

In a medium bowl, combine the ground sirloin, cooked brown rice, onion, marjoram, salt, and pepper. Firmly stuff the mixture into the green peppers; mound the tops if necessary.

Combine the tomato soup and water in the prepared baking dish. Set the stuffed peppers into the dish. Cover the whole dish with aluminum foil and bake for 30 minutes. Uncover and bake for about 15 minutes longer, until a meat thermometer inserted in the filling reads 160°F. Baste occasionally with the sauce during cooking. Spoon the sauce over the stuffed peppers and serve immediately.

NUTRITIONAL CONTENT PER SERVING: **Calories: 325   Protein: 15 g Carbohydrates: 54 g   Fat: 6 g   Saturated fat: 1 g   Cholesterol: 26 mg Sodium: 473 mg   Fiber: 3 g   17 percent calories from fat**

Beef and Broccoli Stir-fry

Firefighter David W. Durbin
Tenopah Test Range
Nevada

Serves 6

Lean beef is not a dangerous food if eaten in moderation. In fact, it is a good source of protein and iron and is not particularly high in fat. When mixed with broccoli in this Asian-influenced stir-fry, it is sensational. This is a good way to enjoy a fondness for beef: Eat small amounts and pair it with larger quantities of other foods you like such as rice and broccoli.

3 tablespoons low-sodium soy sauce

3 tablespoons dry sherry

2 teaspoons grated fresh ginger

1 clove garlic, minced

¼ teaspoon ground red pepper

1 tablespoon cornstarch

1 pound round steak, cut into ½-by-2-inch strips

2 tablespoons canola or other vegetable oil

1 medium onion, thinly sliced

1 bunch broccoli, cut into florets

2 cups beef broth, preferably homemade (page 112), or canned low-sodium broth

4 cups hot cooked rice

In a small bowl, combine the soy sauce, sherry, ginger, garlic, and ground red pepper. Whisk in the cornstarch until dissolved. Add the beef strips, mix well, and let them marinate at room temperature for at least 10 minutes but no longer than 30 minutes. Or marinate in the refrigerator for up to 4 hours.

In a large nonstick skillet, heat 1 tablespoon of the oil over medium-high heat. Remove the beef strips from the marinade, reserving the marinade. Stir-fry the beef for about 2 minutes, until rare. Transfer to a plate and set aside.

Heat the remaining 1 tablespoon of oil in the skillet. Add the onion and broccoli and stir-fry for 1 minute. Add the beef broth, cover, and cook for about 3 minutes, until the broccoli is crisp-tender.

Add the beef strips with the reserved marinade and cook until the sauce thickens. Serve immediately with the hot rice.

NUTRITIONAL CONTENT PER SERVING: **Calories: 275   Protein: 15 g Carbohydrates: 39 g   Fat: 6 g   Saturated fat: 2 g   Cholesterol: 25 mg Sodium: 814 mg   Fiber: 3 g   20 percent calories from fat**

Truckie Veal and Peppers

Firefighter Thomas Mott and Nancy Mott
Ladder Company 129
New York City Fire Department
Flushing, New York

Serves 6 to 8

I use the term "truckie" several times in the book. It's NYFD slang for a firefighter assigned to a ladder company, as I am. It's our job to gain access to the fire building, ventilate it, and search for possible victims. Not surprisingly, there is a friendly rivalry between ladder companies and engine companies. Engine members brag that their job, to get water on the fire, is the most important, and we claim otherwise! I have been in engine companies and ladder companies, and I know I have never quenched a fire with an ax and never forced a door with a hose. Both jobs are vitally important, and we are all gratefully dependent on one another, often for our lives. Tom and I have been truckies since my assignment to Ladder Company 129. This is a terrific recipe that he and his wife came up with for this book.

3 pounds veal shoulder, cut in 2-inch pieces
1 large onion, sliced
2 red bell peppers, quartered and seeded
2 green bell peppers, quartered and seeded
2 cloves garlic, thinly sliced
2 cups dry red wine
6 cups beef broth, preferably homemade (page 112), or canned
    low-sodium broth
One 28-ounce can peeled Italian plum tomatoes, drained

2 teaspoons Italian herb seasoning
½ teaspoon salt
¼ teaspoon crushed hot red pepper flakes
1 pound orzo (rice-shaped pasta)
2 tablespoons cornstarch
1 cup cold water

Spray a large nonstick skillet with nonstick cooking spray and heat over medium-high heat. In as many batches as necessary, cook the veal cubes for about 8 minutes per batch, turning often, until they are browned on all sides. Transfer to a large Dutch oven.

Spray the skillet again with nonstick cooking spray. Add the onion, bell peppers, and garlic and cook over medium heat, covered, for about 5 minutes, until the vegetables soften. Stir in the red wine and bring the mixture to a simmer.

Transfer the vegetable mixture to the Dutch oven. Add the beef broth, tomatoes, herb seasoning, salt, and red pepper flakes and bring to a simmer. Stir with a spoon to break up the tomatoes. Reduce the heat to low and simmer for 2 to 2½ hours, until the veal is very tender.

Shortly before serving, bring a large pot of lightly salted water to a boil, add the orzo, and cook it for about 6 minutes, until it is barely tender. Drain well.

In a small bowl, whisk the cornstarch with the water until the cornstarch is dissolved. Stir the cornstarch into the simmering stew and cook for about 1 minute more, until the sauce thickens. Serve immediately with the hot orzo.

NUTRITIONAL CONTENT PER SERVING: **Calories: 471   Protein: 28 g**
Carbohydrates: 54 g   Fat: 16 g   Saturated fat: 5 g   Cholesterol: 83 mg
Sodium: 96 mg   Fiber: 5 g   30 percent calories from fat

Pizza and Breads

Firehouse Pizza

We eat a lot of Sicilian-style pizza in New York, which is usually baked in a rectangle and has thicker crust and more filling than traditional pizza pie. Some people call it deep-dish pizza or Chicago-style pizza (we never use the latter term in the Big Apple!). As much as we like round pizza, a hefty slice of Sicilian hits the spot.

I like to make it because the crust requires no rolling out. You just press it into a rectangular pan and spoon the topping over it. The topping I suggest here is meaty, but you can customize your own by adding sausage or chopped vegetables. You can also use the Old-Fashioned Tomato Pasta Sauce on page 116. Finally, if you don't have time to make pizza dough, spread this sauce on Boboli or commercially made pizza dough from the supermarket. Either way, it's much lower in fat than the pizza from the joint on the corner.

WHOLE WHEAT CRUST

1 package dry active yeast
½ teaspoon sugar
¼ cup warm (100° to 110°F) water
¾ cup cold water
2 cups unbleached all-purpose flour
⅔ cup whole wheat flour
1 teaspoon salt

BEEF AND MUSHROOM TOPPING

8 ounces lean ground sirloin
1 medium onion, chopped
5 ounces fresh mushrooms, thinly sliced

2 cloves garlic, minced

1½ cups tomato puree

2 tablespoons tomato paste

1 teaspoon dried basil

1 teaspoon dried oregano

¼ teaspoon crushed hot red pepper flakes

1½ cups shredded part-skim mozzarella cheese

To make the crust, in a glass measuring cup, dissolve the yeast and sugar in the warm water. Let stand for about 5 minutes, until the mixture begins to swell and foam. Stir in the cold water.

In a food processor fitted with the metal blade, pulse the flours and salt. With the machine running, add the yeast mixture through the feed tube in a steady stream. Process until the dough forms a ball on top of the blade. (If the dough is too wet or too dry, it will not form a ball. Feel the dough; if it is sticky and wet, add more flour, 2 tablespoons at a time. Process after each addition, until the dough forms a ball. If the dough is crumbly and dry, add more water, 1 tablespoon at a time. Process after each addition, until the dough forms a ball.)

To knead the dough, process the ball of dough for 45 seconds.

Once the dough is kneaded, gather it into a ball and transfer it to a lightly oiled, medium glass or ceramic bowl. Turn the dough in the bowl to coat it with oil. Cover the bowl tightly with plastic wrap and let it rise in a warm place for about 1 hour, until it has doubled in volume.

To make the topping, spray a medium nonstick skillet with nonstick cooking spray. Add the ground beef, onion, mushrooms, and garlic and cook over medium-high heat for about 5 minutes, stirring occasionally, until the meat loses its pink color and the vegetables are softened. Drain off any fat. Stir in the

continued

tomato puree, tomato paste, basil, oregano, and red pepper flakes. Bring to a simmer, reduce the heat to low, and cook for about 5 minutes, until the sauce has thickened. Remove from the heat and cool completely.

Preheat the oven to 450°F. Spray a 15-by-10-inch jelly-roll pan with non-stick cooking spray.

Punch down the risen dough and knead it briefly on a lightly floured work surface. Pat and stretch the dough into the pan to the size of the pan. Cover with plastic wrap and let stand in a warm place for about 20 minutes, until puffy. Spread the cooled topping evenly over the dough, leaving a ½-inch border around the edges. Sprinkle with the cheese.

Bake for 18 to 20 minutes, until the cheese melts and the crust is lightly browned. Cool slightly before cutting into rectangles to serve.

NOTE: If you don't have a food processor, make the dough by hand. Combine the flours and salt in a large bowl. Make a well in the center, and add the yeast mixture. Working from the inside of the well, blend the flour with the liquid, mixing in more flour until the dough is stiff. Add more flour or water if the dough is too wet or too dry. Turn the dough out onto a floured work surface and knead for about 10 minutes, until it is smooth and elastic. Proceed with the recipe by letting the dough rise.

NUTRITIONAL CONTENT PER SERVING: **Calories: 570 Protein: 9 g
Carbohydrates: 126 g Fat: 5 g Saturated fat: 2 g Cholesterol: 159 mg
Sodium: 786 mg Fiber: 3 g 7 percent calories from fat**

Pumpkin Bread

Firefighter Phil Wigglesworth
Engine Company 32
Washington, D.C., Fire Department
Washington, D.C.

Makes 2 loaves

This quick bread is a good one to have on hand anytime—it makes a nutritious snack with a glass of milk or cup of coffee. The pumpkin moistens the bread and also provides a good share of beta carotene.

2 cups sugar
2 large eggs
2 large egg whites
1 cup unsweetened applesauce
2 cups canned unsweetened pumpkin puree
3½ cups all-purpose flour
1 teaspoon baking powder
1 teaspoon ground cinnamon
1 teaspoon ground allspice
1 teaspoon grated nutmeg
2 teaspoons baking soda
1 teaspoon salt
½ teaspoon ground cloves
⅔ cup unsweetened apple juice
1 cup raisins or dried cranberries

continued

P reheat the oven to 350°F. Lightly grease and flour two 9-by-5-inch loaf pans. Tap out any excess flour.

I n a medium bowl, combine the sugar, eggs, egg whites, and applesauce. With a handheld electric mixer at high speed, beat for about 3 minutes, until the mixture is light and fluffy. Stir in the pumpkin.

I n another bowl, whisk together the flour, baking powder, cinnamon, all-spice, nutmeg, baking soda, salt, and cloves. Stir the dry mixture into the pumpkin batter. Add the apple juice and raisins and mix well.

D ivide the batter evenly between the loaf pans. Bake for 65 to 75 minutes, until a toothpick inserted into the center of the bread comes out clean. Remove from the oven and let stand for 10 minutes, then invert and unmold onto wire baking racks to cool completely.

NUTRITIONAL CONTENT PER SERVING: **(1 serving = one ½-inch slice)**
Calories: 113   Protein: 2 g   Carbohydrates: 26 g   Fat: 0 g   Saturated fat: 0 g
Cholesterol: 12 mg   Sodium: 125 mg   Fiber: 1 g   4 percent calories from fat

W hole Wheat Banana Bread

Makes 1 loaf

B anana bread is an old favorite with many people, and because bananas are available all year long, it's one you can make whenever you have a hankering for a moist, sweet bread. This one is extra moist because I use applesauce as well as bananas. And the egg whites do the binding without adding cholesterol.

1½ cups all-purpose flour
1 cup whole wheat flour
2 teaspoons baking powder
1 teaspoon baking soda
1 teaspoon ground cinnamon
¼ teaspoon salt
6 ripe bananas, mashed
1 cup sugar
½ cup unsweetened applesauce
3 large egg whites
1 teaspoon vanilla extract
½ cup finely chopped walnuts

Preheat the oven to 350°F. Spray a 9-by-5-inch loaf pan with nonstick cooking spray.

In a medium bowl, whisk the flours, baking powder, baking soda, cinnamon, and salt to combine.

In another medium bowl, beat the mashed bananas, sugar, applesauce, egg whites, and vanilla until well mixed. Add the dry ingredients and whisk just until smooth. Stir in the walnuts. Transfer the batter to the loaf pan and smooth the top.

Bake for 50 minutes to 1 hour, until the top is browned and the sides of the bread pull away from the sides of the pan. Remove from the oven and let stand for 10 minutes on a wire baking rack. Invert and unmold onto the rack, turn right side up, and let cool completely.

NUTRITIONAL CONTENT PER SERVING: (**1 serving = one ½-inch slice**)
Calories: 222   Protein: 6 g   Carbohydrates: 54 g   Fat: 1 g   Saturated fat: 0 g
Cholesterol: 0 mg   Sodium: 159 mg   Fiber: 5 g   3 percent calories from fat

Zucchini Bread

Firefighter Lisa Peck
Community Fire Company
North Grosvenordale, Connecticut

Makes 1 loaf

In this recipe Connecticut firefighter Lisa Peck relies on zucchini and applesauce for moisture and flavor. I wouldn't be surprised if Lisa had a garden, since I don't know a gardener who doesn't make zucchini bread many times over in the late summer when the prolific squash seems to overtake all other vegetables. It's lucky for us, because this low-fat quick bread is wonderful.

1 large zucchini, diced but not peeled
1 cup granulated sugar
½ cup liquid egg substitute or 2 large eggs
½ cup unsweetened applesauce
¾ teaspoon vanilla extract
1¼ cups all-purpose flour
½ cup whole wheat flour
¾ teaspoon baking soda
¾ teaspoon baking powder
½ teaspoon ground cinnamon
½ teaspoon salt
¼ teaspoon ground ginger
¼ teaspoon ground allspice
¼ teaspoon ground cloves
½ cup coarsely chopped walnuts

Preheat the oven to 350°F. Lightly grease and flour a 9-by-5-inch loaf pan. Tap out any excess flour.

In a blender or food processor fitted with the metal blade, combine the zucchini, sugar, egg substitute, applesauce, and vanilla and blend until smooth. Pour into a large bowl.

In a medium bowl, whisk the flours, baking soda, baking powder, cinnamon, salt, ginger, allspice, and cloves until combined. Add the combined dry ingredients to the liquid and whisk until just combined. Stir in the walnuts.

Pour the batter into the loaf pan and bake for 50 minutes to 1 hour, until the sides of the bread begin to pull away from the sides of the pan. Remove from the oven and let stand for 10 minutes on a wire baking rack. Invert and unmold onto the rack, turn right side up, and let cool completely.

NUTRITIONAL CONTENT PER SERVING (USING EGG SUBSTITUTE):

(1 serving = one ½-inch slice)

Calories: 202   Protein: 4 g   Carbohydrates: 40 g   Fat: 3 g   Saturated fat: 1 g

Cholesterol: 42 mg   Sodium: 205 mg   Fiber: 1 g   14 percent calories from fat

Cynthia's Sweet Potato Buns

Makes 12 buns

This is a quick and foolproof recipe for some filling buns that turn the lightest meal into a treat. It combines a baking mix, such as Bisquick, with vitamin-rich sweet potatoes, so that you can mix these up in no time. Just remember to allow plenty of time to bake and cool the potatoes. The softness of the dough depends on the moisture of the sweet potatoes, so take care not to add too much milk.

2 to 3 sweet potatoes (about 1 pound), scrubbed
2⅔ cups dry buttermilk baking mix
⅓ cup packed brown sugar
Scant ½ cup skim milk

Preheat the oven to 400°F. Place the potatoes on a sheet of aluminum foil and bake for about 45 minutes, until they are tender. Remove from the oven and let cool.

Peel the cooled potatoes, transfer them to a large bowl, and mash with a fork. Stir in the buttermilk baking mixture and brown sugar. Add just enough milk to form a soft dough.

Flour a work surface, spread the dough on it, and pat it to ½-inch thickness. Using a 2½-inch round cookie cutter or upturned glass, stamp out 12 buns. Don't twist the cutter as you lift it from the dough.

Place the buns on an ungreased baking sheet and bake for 15 to 20 minutes, until they are golden brown.

NUTRITIONAL CONTENT PER SERVING: **(1 serving = 1 bun)**

Calories: 148   Protein: 2 g   Carbohydrates: 29 g   Fat: 3 g   Saturated fat: 1 g

Cholesterol: 0 mg   Sodium: 268 mg   Fiber: 1 g   18 percent calories from fat

Luigi's Irish Soda Bread

Firefighter Louis Minutoli
Ladder Company 129
New York City Fire Department
Flushing, New York

Makes 1 loaf

You may get a kick out of the fact that a guy named Minutoli makes some of the best Irish soda bread going—but that's New York! This loaf is fun to make because you bake it in a skillet (make sure the skillet is ovenproof—no plastic handle) and then cut it into wedges for serving.

4 cups all-purpose flour
½ cup sugar
1 tablespoon baking powder
⅛ teaspoon salt
½ cup canola or other vegetable oil
2 cups low-fat milk
1 cup raisins

continued

Preheat the oven to 300°F.

In a large bowl, using a pastry blender or 2 knives, mix the flour, sugar, baking powder, and salt with the oil until grainy. Add 1 cup of the milk and the raisins and mix well. Gradually add more milk until the batter sticks together.

Shape the batter into an 8-inch ball and place the ball in an ungreased medium oven-proof skillet. Flatten the dough gently so that it fills the skillet. With a knife, cut a shallow cross in the top of the dough. Bake for 1 hour, until the bread is browned and a toothpick inserted in it comes out clean. Remove from the oven and let stand for about 10 minutes before turning out onto a wire baking rack to cool completely. Cut the bread into wedges to serve.

NUTRITIONAL CONTENT PER SERVING: (1 serving = one 1½-inch wedge)
Calories: 473   Protein: 8 g   Carbohydrates: 78 g   Fat: 15 g   Saturated fat: 1 g
Cholesterol: 1 mg   Sodium: 206 mg   Fiber: 3 g   28 percent calories from fat

Zucchini Loaf LaClair

Firefighter Kevin LaClair and Stephanie LaClair   Serves 12
Ladder Company 129
New York City Fire Department
Flushing, New York

Before my current assignment to Ladder Company 129, I was temporarily assigned for thirty days to Ladder Company 151 in Forest Hills, Queens. The captain of the company, Gerald LaClair, requested that I stay on, and my tour extended to seven months. I was sorry when the months were over, but within weeks of my permanent assignment to 129, Captain LaClair's son, Kevin, was assigned to my firehouse. Kevin is as much of a pleasure to work with as his father is, and his wife, Stephanie, is an excellent cook. She contributed this recipe for a savory loaf that is very good for brunch, although it also makes a nice weekday supper too.

1 cup dry buttermilk baking mix
½ cup grated Parmesan cheese
1 tablespoon chopped fresh parsley
1 clove garlic, minced
½ teaspoon dried oregano
½ teaspoon salt
⅛ teaspoon black pepper
¾ cup liquid egg substitute
½ cup skim milk
½ cup finely chopped onion
3 cups thinly sliced zucchini (3 or 4 small zucchini)

Preheat the oven to 350°F. Lightly spray a 13-by-9-inch baking pan with nonstick cooking spray.

In a medium bowl, combine the buttermilk baking mix, Parmesan cheese, parsley, garlic, oregano, salt, and pepper and whisk together. Add the liquid egg substitute and milk and mix just until smooth. Fold in the onion and sliced zucchini. Transfer to the baking pan and smooth the top.

Bake for 25 to 30 minutes, until the top is golden brown and a toothpick inserted in the center of the loaf comes out clean. Let cool slightly before serving.

NUTRITIONAL CONTENT PER SERVING: Calories: 161   Protein: 10 g
Carbohydrates: 17 g   Fat: 5 g   Saturated fat: 2 g   Cholesterol: 7 mg
Sodium: 634 mg   Fiber: 1 g   30 percent calories from fat

Side Dishes

# Hummus

Hummus is a filling, healthful snack to have on hand to take the place of onion or cheese dips. It also makes a good side dish with light foods. With a food processor, it's made in a flash and will keep in the refrigerator for a couple of days. I like it on cucumber slices, but it makes a good dip for pita bread and plain crackers and is also a terrific sandwich spread. This recipe does not call for olive oil, as many others do, although there is fat in tahini—a ground sesame paste sold in Asian markets and most grocery stores.

One 15-ounce can garbanzo beans (chickpeas), undrained
3 tablespoons tahini
2 tablespoons fresh lemon juice
1 clove garlic, minced
½ cup chicken broth, garbanzo bean liquid, or water
3 tablespoons chopped fresh parsley
1 teaspoon salt
Ground red pepper or cayenne
2 cucumbers, peeled and sliced ¼ inch thick

Drain the garbanzo beans and reserve the liquid (if using instead of chicken broth). Rinse the beans, drain again, and discard the rinse water.

In a blender or food processor fitted with a metal blade, combine the garbanzo beans, tahini, lemon juice, and garlic. Gradually add the chicken broth, garbanzo bean liquid, or water through the work tube to make a smooth, thick puree.

$\mathbb{P}$rocess until smooth. Scrape down the sides of the food processor work bowl as needed. Transfer to a serving bowl and stir in the parsley, salt, and red pepper. Serve with cucumber slices for dipping.

NUTRITIONAL CONTENT PER SERVING: **Calories: 109** **Protein: 4 g**
Carbohydrates: 16 g **Fat: 4 g** **Saturated fat: 1 g** **Cholesterol: 0 mg**
Sodium: 161 mg **Fiber: 4 g** **31 percent calories from fat**

Spinach Cheese Bake

Firefighter Joseph Aquino and Debbie Aquino

Serves 6

Engine Company 42

New York City Fire Department

Bronx, New York (Retired to Montana)

Frozen spinach is much easier to work with than fresh and is a good item to have on hand in the freezer. (Fresh spinach is great, but it has to be washed very thoroughly, and you need a lot to feed six hungry firefighters.) I like to serve this side dish with grilled meat or fish, but it also makes an acceptable vegetarian main course.

2 tablespoons dried Italian-seasoned bread crumbs

2 cups low-fat cottage cheese

3 large egg whites

⅓ cup all-purpose flour

1 teaspoon dried basil

1 clove garlic, minced

Pinch of freshly ground black pepper

Two 10-ounce packages chopped frozen spinach, thawed and squeezed
    dry

1 cup grated part-skim mozzarella cheese

Preheat the oven to 350°F. Spray a 9-inch round pie plate with nonstick cooking spray. Sprinkle the pie plate with the bread crumbs and tilt gently to distribute the crumbs evenly. Tap out excess crumbs.

In a food processor, blend the cottage cheese and egg whites until smooth. Add the flour, basil, garlic, and pepper. Mix well. Add the spinach and mozzarella and pulse to combine.

Spoon the mixture into the prepared pie plate and set the pie plate on a baking sheet. Bake for about 40 minutes, until the spinach mixture is puffed and browned. Serve hot.

NUTRITIONAL CONTENT PER SERVING: **Calories: 179   Protein: 20 g Carbohdrates: 16 g   Fat: 4 g   Saturated fat: 2 g   Cholesterol: 14 mg Sodium: 627 mg   Fiber: 3 g   21 percent calories from fat**

Idaho Tacos

Captain Joseph Bledsoe
Health and Fitness Center
Phoenix Fire Department
Phoenix, Arizona

Serves 2

Baked potatoes are a great source of carbohydrates without being a source of fat or calories. One potato has only about 90 calories. Here is a way to serve them with a southwestern flair, a recipe donated by a firefighter from Arizona, where they no doubt use "hot" salsa. You can select the amount of heat you want by the type of salsa you buy. The pinto beans provide protein and fiber, as well as most of the calories. I like these as a light meal in themselves, but they also make a good and filling side dish.

2 large baking potatoes, scrubbed
One 8-ounce can pinto beans, drained and rinsed
½ cup prepared salsa
½ cup (2 ounces) shredded low-fat, low-sodium Cheddar cheese

Preheat the oven to 425°F. Put the potatoes on a baking sheet and bake for about 1 hour, until they are tender when pierced with a sharp knife.

Meanwhile, in a medium saucepan, bring the pinto beans and salsa to a simmer over medium heat, stirring often.

Remove the potatoes from the oven and let them cool for about 2 minutes. Split them lengthwise. Press the ends of the potatoes inward to fluff up the insides. Put each potato into a shallow bowl, spoon half of the hot beans and salsa on top of each, and sprinkle each with cheese. Serve immediately.

NUTRITIONAL CONTENT PER SERVING: Calories: 416   Protein: 20 g
Carbohydrates: 79 g   Fat: 3 g   Saturated fat: 1 g   Cholesterol: 6 mg
Sodium: 258 mg   Fiber: 16 g   6 percent calories from fat

Hell's Hundred Acres Sweet Potato Fries

Firefighter James Moerschel   Serves 8
Forensic Unit
New York City Fire Department
New York, New York

When Jim first joined the NYFD, he was assigned to Ladder Company 5, a unit that responded to fires in the area of lower Manhattan we now call SoHo and Tribeca. In the 1950s and '60s the area was dubbed Hell's Hundred Acres by the firefighters who had to battle the ferocious fires that broke out in the area's cavernous warehouses and loft buildings. These four- and five-alarmers took the lives of many firefighters and injured many more. The large, poorly maintained buildings often housed sweatshops, were not fitted with sprinkler systems, and, to make matters worse, had basements and subcellars where fires could rage out of control. Jim now works as a photographer for the Forensic Unit, aiding arson investigations and legal disputes. This recipe is Jim's substitute for greasy french fries. It's made with beta carotene–rich sweet potatoes and very little oil. The potatoes are baked, not fried—and they taste great!

continued

4 sweet potatoes, peeled

2 tablespoons canola or other vegetable oil

2 tablespoons Cajun spice seasoning

1 teaspoon hot red pepper sauce

Preheat the oven to 400°F. Spray a large baking sheet with nonstick cooking spray.

Cut the sweet potatoes into ½-by-3-inch strips. Put them in a large bowl and toss with the oil, seasoning, and hot sauce until well coated.

Spread the potatoes on the baking sheet and bake for about 40 minutes, turning occasionally, until tender. Serve immediately.

NUTRITIONAL CONTENT PER SERVING: **Calories: 108   Protein: 1 g   Carbohydrates: 18 g   Fat: 4 g   Saturated fat: 0 g   Cholesterol: 0 mg   Sodium: 277 mg   Fiber: 2 g   30 percent calories from fat**

High-Energy Scalloped Potatoes

Serves 8

You may think of scalloped potatoes as an old-fashioned dish, swimming in butter and cream—exactly the way we do not want to eat spuds today! These are anything but. They are made with low-fat cheese and skim milk and taste unlike the potatoes you may remember. They taste *better.*

¼ cup finely chopped onion

3 tablespoons all-purpose flour

½ teaspoon salt

¼ teaspoon black pepper

2 pounds baking potatoes (about 6 potatoes), peeled and sliced ⅛ inch thick

½ cup (about 2 ounces) shredded low-fat Cheddar cheese

2½ cups skim milk, scalded

½ teaspoon paprika

Preheat the oven to 350°F. Spray a 13-by-9-inch baking dish with nonstick cooking spray.

In a small bowl, mix the onion, flour, salt, and pepper.

Arrange a third of the potatoes in the baking dish. Sprinkle with half of the onion mixture and half of the cheese. Top with half of the remaining potatoes, then sprinkle with the remaining onions and cheese. Use the remaining potatoes to make a final layer. Pour the scalded milk over the potatoes and sprinkle with the paprika. Cover tightly with aluminum foil.

Bake for 30 minutes. Uncover and bake for about 1 hour, until the potatoes are tender. Let stand for 5 minutes before serving.

NUTRITIONAL CONTENT PER SERVING: **Calories: 165   Protein: 6 g**
Carbohydrates: 35 g   Fat: 0 g   Saturated fat: 0 g   Cholesterol: 1 mg
Sodium: 87 mg   Fiber: 3 g   2 percent calories from fat

Five-Carb Casserole

Sweet potatoes are wonderful combined with fruit. The combination is satisfyingly sweet without being cloying or even dessertlike. I call this "five-carb" because the fruit provides good complex carbohydrates, as do the sweet potatoes. Try this at Thanksgiving instead of candied sweet potatoes—you'll love it.

One 48-ounce can sweet potatoes (not in syrup), drained and sliced ½ inch thick
4 tart apples (such as Granny Smith), cored, peeled, and sliced ½ inch thick
Two 16-ounce cans unsweetened sliced pineapple, juice reserved
4 bananas, peeled and sliced
Two 16-ounce cans jellied cranberry sauce, sliced in rounds ½ inch thick
½ cup packed light brown sugar
½ teaspoon ground cinnamon

Preheat the oven to 350°F. Lightly spray a 13-by-9-inch baking dish with nonstick cooking spray.

Layer a third of the sweet potatoes in the bottom of the prepared baking dish. Continue layering with half of the apples, pineapple, bananas, and cranberry sauce. Sprinkle with half of the brown sugar and cinnamon. Layer with another third of the sweet potatoes, then top with the remaining apples, pineapple, bananas, cranberry sauce, brown sugar, and cinnamon. Top with the remaining sweet potatoes. Pour the reserved pineapple juice over the whole casserole.

Cover with aluminum foil and bake for 15 minutes. Uncover and bake for another 15 minutes, until the casserole is hot and bubbling. Serve immediately.

NUTRITIONAL CONTENT PER SERVING: **Calories: 368**   **Protein: 3 g**
Carbohydrates: 92 g   **Fat: 1 g**   **Saturated fat: 0 g**   **Cholesterol: 0 mg**
Sodium: 86 mg   **Fiber: 7 g**   **2 percent calories from fat**

Whole Wheat Vegetable Stuffing

This stuffing has no oil, margarine, or butter. I use chicken broth to moisten the bread cubes and lots of vegetables and herbs for flavor. The recipe makes enough for a 10- to 15-pound turkey or three 5- to 6-pound roasting chickens. Never stuff poultry until just before you are ready to roast it—and once the bird and stuffing are cooked, remove the stuffing and store leftovers in a separate container.

1 cup chicken broth, preferably homemade (page 110), or canned
    low-sodium broth
1 onion, chopped
3 stalks celery, chopped
2 carrots, shredded
8 ounces mushrooms, sliced
½ cup chopped fresh parsley
¼ cup chopped fresh dill
1½ teaspoons dried savory
1 teaspoon dried sage
1 teaspoon salt
½ teaspoon grated nutmeg
¼ teaspoon black pepper
8 cups day-old whole wheat bread cubes (about 10 to 12 slices cut in
    ½-inch cubes)

In a large skillet, bring the broth, onion, celery, carrots, and mushrooms to a simmer over medium heat. Reduce the heat to low, cover, and simmer for about 6 minutes, until the vegetables soften. Transfer the vegetables to a large bowl and stir in the parsley, dill, savory, sage, salt, nutmeg, and pepper.

Add the bread cubes and toss well. Use the stuffing for turkey, chicken, or fish. Alternatively, bake it, uncovered, in a lightly buttered casserole for about 30 minutes in a preheated 350°F oven.

NUTRITIONAL CONTENT PER SERVING: **Calories: 100   Protein: 5 g Carbohydrates: 19 g   Fat: 2 g   Saturated fat: 1 g   Cholesterol: 0 mg Sodium: 515 mg   Fiber: 4 g   14 percent calories from fat**

Vegetable-Stuffed Zucchini

Stuffing zucchini shells with a mixture of mushrooms, zucchini, and bread crumbs is a good way to use the plentiful squash. Come September, most gardens are overstocked with it. This is not only a great side dish but also a fine vegetarian main course.

4 zucchini, cut in half lengthwise
1 tablespoon olive oil
4 ounces fresh mushrooms, chopped
1 scallion, chopped
1 clove garlic, minced
½ cup fresh bread crumbs
1 teaspoon dried savory
½ teaspoon salt
⅛ teaspoon black pepper
Two 5-ounce cans Italian-seasoned stewed tomatoes
½ cup (about 2 ounces) shredded part-skim mozzarella cheese

Preheat the oven to 350°F. Lightly spray the inside of a 13-by-9-inch baking dish with nonstick cooking spray.

With a spoon, scoop out the insides of the zucchini, leaving a shell about ¼ inch thick. Chop the scooped-out zucchini flesh.

In a large nonstick skillet, heat the oil over medium heat and cook the chopped zucchini, mushrooms, scallion, and garlic, covered, for about 5 minutes, stirring occasionally, until the mushrooms soften.

Uncover and cook for about 3 minutes longer, until all the liquid given off by the mushrooms evaporates and the vegetables begin to brown. Stir in the bread crumbs, savory, salt, and pepper.

Arrange the zucchini shells in the prepared dish. Stuff the shells with the bread mixture. Pour the stewed tomatoes around the zucchini. Cover with aluminum foil and bake for about 25 minutes, until the zucchini are just tender. Uncover, sprinkle the tops with the cheese, and bake for 5 minutes more, until the cheese melts. Spoon the tomatoes over the zucchini and serve immediately.

NUTRITIONAL CONTENT PER SERVING: Calories: 87   Protein: 5
Carbohydrates: 12 g   Fat: 3 g   Saturated fat: 1 g   Cholesterol: 4 mg
Sodium: 271 mg   Fiber: 4 g   31 percent calories from fat

Coffin-Cut Eggplant Gyros

I call these gyros "coffin-cut" because when you are inspecting for the spread of fire under a flat, internal roof or trying to reach a fire under the roof so that you can douse it with water, you cut a large, rectangular hole in the roof about the size of a coffin. For this gyro, you cut the pita bread open, fill it with a vegetarian mixture of eggplant and bread crumbs, and "douse" your hunger.

1 large eggplant, peeled and sliced ½ inch thick
1 tablespoon salt
3 large egg whites
1 cup dried Italian-seasoned bread crumbs
4 pita breads, sliced to form pockets
1 large tomato, sliced
1 red onion, thinly sliced
1 bunch fresh spinach leaves, well rinsed, stems removed
1 cup plain nonfat yogurt

Preheat the oven to 350°F. Place a large piece of aluminum foil in a 13-by-9-inch baking dish and crumple it slightly.

In a large colander, toss the eggplant slices with the salt. Let the eggplant drain for 30 minutes. Rinse well under cold water and pat dry with paper towels.

In a medium bowl, beat the egg whites lightly. Place the bread crumbs in a shallow plate. Dip the eggplant slices into the egg whites and then into the crumbs; pat to help the crumbs adhere.

Arrange the eggplant slices on the crumpled aluminum foil. Bake for 15 minutes, turn, and bake for about 5 minutes more, until lightly browned and tender.

Divide the eggplant into 4 equal portions and stuff a portion into each of the pitas. Divide the tomato and onion slices and spinach into 4 equal portions and stuff a portion of each into the pitas. Drizzle each pita with the yogurt and serve immediately.

NUTRITIONAL CONTENT PER SERVING: **Calories: 460   Protein: 27 g Carbohydrates: 85 g   Fat: 3 g   Saturated fat: 1 g   Cholesterol: 3 mg Sodium: 764 mg   Fiber: 14 g   6 percent calories from fat**

The Lieutenant's Stuffed Mushrooms

Lieutenant Donald Struck
Engine Company 5
Linden Fire Department
Linden, New Jersey

Makes 16 stuffed mushrooms

Buy the biggest white mushrooms you can find for these stuffed mushrooms. Don't rinse them under running water, but instead wipe them clean with a damp cloth. These are a nice side dish with grilled meat and chicken, and they also make good hors d'oeuvres.

16 large mushrooms
2 teaspoons olive oil
1 onion, finely chopped
1 clove garlic, minced
1 cup dried seasoned bread crumbs
¼ cup liquid egg substitute
2 tablespoons chopped fresh parsley

Preheat the oven to 350°F. Spray a baking sheet with nonstick cooking spray.

Remove the stems from the mushrooms. Reserve the caps and chop the stems finely.

In a medium nonstick skillet, heat the oil over medium heat. Add the chopped mushroom stems, onion, and garlic. Cover and cook for about 5 minutes, until the mushrooms soften.

Remove the cover and cook for 3 to 4 minutes more, until the liquid given off by the mushrooms has evaporated to about 2 tablespoons. Transfer to a medium bowl and let cool. Stir in the bread crumbs and liquid egg substitute.

Stuff the mushroom caps with the bread crumb mixture. Place on the prepared baking sheet and bake for 15 to 20 minutes, until the tops are browned. Sprinkle with the parsley and serve immediately.

NUTRITIONAL CONTENT PER SERVING: **(1 serving = 1 stuffed mushroom)**

Calories: 75   Protein: 3 g   Carbohydrates: 11 g   Fat: 3 g   Saturated fat: 1 g

Cholesterol: 22 mg   Sodium: 82 mg   Fiber: 1 g   29 percent calories from fat

Desserts

Blue Ribbon Carrot Cake

Serves 16

I try to tell firefighters that adopting healthy eating habits doesn't mean they can never have ice cream, cake, or beer again. As long as eating and fitness habits are on target most of the time, there is room for an occasional indulgence. The following dessert proved to my fellow firefighters how good low-fat cooking can be. I won the 1993 NYFD Bake-Off with this carrot cake, which gets less than 30 percent of its calories from fat.

CARROT CAKE
1 cup pitted prunes
2½ cups sifted cake flour
2 teaspoons ground cinnamon
2 teaspoons baking powder
1½ teaspoons baking soda
1 teaspoon salt
2 large eggs
2 large egg whites
2 cups sugar
⅓ cup vegetable oil
5 to 6 small carrots, peeled and grated
One 8-ounce can crushed pineapple, drained

CREAM CHEESE FROSTING
12 ounces low-fat cream cheese, softened
½ cup confectioner's sugar
1½ teaspoons vanilla extract

Preheat the oven to 350°F.

In a food processor, combine the pitted prunes with 6 tablespoons of hot water and process until smooth. Set aside.

Coat the inside of two 8-inch square or 9-inch round cake pans with non-stick vegetable spray. Line the bottoms with waxed paper and set aside.

In a medium bowl, stir together the flour, cinnamon, baking powder, baking soda, and salt. In a large bowl, whisk together the eggs and egg whites. Add the sugar, reserved prune puree, and oil and whisk until smooth. Add the dry flour mixture to the egg mixture and stir with a stiff spoon until well blended. Add the carrots and pineapple and stir to blend well.

Divide the batter evenly between the prepared pans and bake for 40 to 50 minutes, until a cake tester inserted in the center comes out clean. Let cool on a wire rack for 10 minutes.

Run a spatula round the edge of the pans to loosen the cakes. Invert the layers onto two plates, peel off the waxed paper, and set the cakes aside to cool completely.

To make the frosting: In a mixing bowl, combine the cream cheese, confectioner's sugar, and vanilla and beat with an electric mixer until smooth. Spread an even layer of frosting over the top of one of the completely cooled cakes. Place the second cake on top of the first and spread the remaining frosting evenly over the top and sides.

NUTRITIONAL CONTENT PER SERVING: (1 serving = one ½-inch wedge)
Calories: 303   Protein: 5 g   Carbohydrates: 52 g   Fat: 9 g   Saturated fat: 3 g
Cholesterol: 38 mg   Sodium: 294 mg   Fiber: 2 g   25 percent calories from fat

Sweet Potato Pie

As you have noticed from the other recipes in this book, I am fond of sweet potatoes—in fact, I sometimes can't seem to get enough of them. They add such great flavor and moisture to baked goods and other dishes that I would, if possible, nominate them to the food hall of fame. And they are packed with beta carotene, which converts to vitamin A in our bodies and helps fight cancer and other diseases. If you haven't tried sweet potato pie, here is your chance.

3 large sweet potatoes (about 2 pounds)
⅓ cup sugar
½ cup evaporated skim milk
¼ cup maple syrup
3 large egg whites
1 tablespoon fresh lemon juice
1 teaspoon ground cinnamon
¼ teaspoon salt
¼ cup raisins
One 9-inch Graham Cracker Pie Shell (page 288)

In a large pot of boiling water, cook the sweet potatoes for about 45 minutes, until they are tender when pierced with a sharp knife. Drain, rinse under cold water, and drain again.

Preheat the oven to 350°F.

When the potatoes are cool enough to handle, peel them and put them in the bowl of an electric mixer. Using a fork or potato masher, coarsely mash the potatoes.

Add the sugar, milk, maple syrup, egg whites, lemon juice, cinnamon, and salt. With the electric mixer set at low speed, beat until the mixture is smooth. Stir in the raisins and pour the mixture into the pie shell.

Bake for about 1 hour, until the pie filling is set and a knife inserted into the center comes out clean. Cool completely on a wire baking rack.

NUTRITIONAL CONTENT PER SERVING: **(1 serving = one 2½-inch wedge)**

Calories: 355   Protein: 6 g   Carbohydrates: 60 g   Fat: 11 g   Saturated fat: 2 g
Cholesterol: 1 mg   Sodium: 352 mg   Fiber: 3 g   27 percent calories from fat

Graham Cracker Pie Shell

Makes one 9-inch pie shell

This crust can be filled with any number of things and can be made up to eight hours before filling. I use it for the Sweet Potato Pie on page 286. Be sure it's cool before filling it.

12 to 14 whole graham crackers
6 tablespoons unsalted butter, melted

Preheat the oven to 350°F.

In a food processor fitted with the metal blade, process the graham crackers until finely ground. Or put the crackers between 2 pieces of waxed paper and crush them with a rolling pin to fine crumbs. You should have about 2½ cups crumbs.

In a small bowl, mix the crumbs and butter until well blended. Press the mixture into a 9-inch pie plate, using the palms of your hands and your fingertips to push the crumbs into the bottom and up the side of the plate. Bake for 7 to 8 minutes, until the crust browns. Cool completely on a wire baking rack before filling.

NUTRITIONAL CONTENT PER SERVING: **(one serving = one 2½-inch wedge)**
Calories: 253   **Protein:** 3 g   **Carbohydrates:** 29 g   **Fat:** 12 g   **Saturated fat:** 6 g
Cholesterol: 23 mg   **Sodium:** 228 mg   **Fiber:** 1 g   **47 percent calories from fat**

The Sponge Cake Sponge

Firefighters are just as concerned about saving a few bucks as everybody else. Most are willing and ready, however, to pitch in the few dollars it costs to buy a meal. Those who are not are affectionately dubbed "seagulls" because, although they don't join in the meal, they wander into the kitchen long after supper is over and scavenge leftovers. One evening a firefighter who likes to bake cooked up a plan to foil our most notorious seagull, and we all cheerfully helped him stage it.

While the seagull was hanging around the kitchen, the baker started raving about the sponge cake he wanted to make. We agreed to help him prepare it, and after the seagull left the kitchen, we watched as the chef took an actual cellulose sponge and positioned it in the cake. He then frosted the cake and marked where the sponge was camouflaged. The rest of us ate big pieces of the real cake, raving about them for hours afterward. The last piece containing the sponge was put away in the refrigerator and the kitchen was darkened for the night. The next morning when we came into the kitchen, we all ran for the garbage. Sure enough, there was the frosted sponge with a huge bite taken out of it! From then on our leftovers were left alone.

Firehouse Mom's Apple Pie

Serves 8

Apple pie is about as traditional as you can get—and what could be more American than Mom's? But this is no conventional apple pie. It has only a top crust, which is lighter and lower in fat and calories than most. I think of this as a pie for the moms of the nineties. And for the firefighters too.

6 large baking apples (such as Granny Smith), peeled, cored, and sliced
    ½ inch thick
1 tablespoon fresh lemon juice
¼ cup plus 1 tablespoon sugar, divided
1 cup plus 2 tablespoons all-purpose flour, divided
½ teaspoon ground cinnamon
⅛ teaspoon ground cloves
¼ cup canola or other vegetable oil
2 tablespoons skim milk

Preheat the oven to 425°F.

In a medium bowl, toss the apples, lemon juice, ¼ cup of the sugar, 2 tablespoons of the flour, the cinnamon, and cloves. Transfer to a 9-inch round pie plate.

In another medium bowl, combine the remaining 1 cup of flour with the oil, milk, and remaining 1 tablespoon of sugar. With a pastry blender, work the ingredients until they are well combined and moist enough to hold together as a dough. Gather the dough into a ball, wrap in plastic, and refrigerate for at least 10 minutes.

Place the dough on a sheet of waxed paper and cover with a second sheet. Roll the dough into a 10-inch round about ⅛ inch thick. If the dough is too firm to roll, let it sit at room temperature for a few minutes. If it is too soft, return it to the refrigerator for a few minutes.

Remove the top sheet of waxed paper and invert the dough onto the apples in the pie plate. Peel off the second sheet of paper. Using your fingers, ease the dough down around the apples inside the pie pan. Turn the edge of the dough under and flute it around the rim of the pie plate. With a knife, make several small slashes in the top of the dough.

Place the pie plate on a baking sheet and bake for 15 minutes. Reduce the temperature to 375°F and continue to bake for 20 to 30 minutes longer, until the crust is golden brown and the filling bubbles. Cool the pie on a wire baking rack. Serve warm or at room temperature.

NUTRITIONAL CONTENT PER SERVING: (1 serving = one 2½-inch wedge)
Calories: 384   Protein: 4 g   Carbohydrates: 61 g   Fat: 15 g   Saturated fat: 1 g
Cholesterol: 0 mg   Sodium: 6 mg   Fiber: 5 g   33 percent calories from fat

High-Rise Sweet Potato Soufflé

Serves 6

New York and other big cities present the challenge of fighting fires in high-rise buildings. We're trained in ways other firefighters may not be, and while we're proud of our abilities, we remain in awe of the destruction a fire in a high-rise can do. But this high-riser is one everyone in my firehouse happily welcomes! The first time they tried it, they could hardly believe it was low in fat and calories. I make it often to convince wary firefighters that good nutrition and low-fat cooking don't require sacrificing taste. The soufflé, which is not a particularly delicate one, is loaded with fiber, carbohydrates, and protein.

3 sweet potatoes (about 1¾ pounds)
2 tablespoons unsalted butter, softened
⅔ cup evaporated skim milk
2 tablespoons all-purpose flour
¼ teaspoon baking powder
½ teaspoon vanilla extract
¼ teaspoon almond extract
⅛ teaspoon salt
3 large egg whites
¼ cup sugar
2 tablespoons packed brown sugar
¼ teaspoon ground cinnamon

In a large pot of boiling water, cook the sweet potatoes for about 45 minutes, until they are tender when pierced with a sharp knife. Drain, rinse under cold water, and drain again.

Preheat the oven to 350°F. Lightly spray a 2-quart baking dish or soufflé dish with nonstick cooking spray.

When the potatoes are cool enough to handle, peel them and put them in the bowl of an electric mixer. Using a fork or potato masher, coarsely mash the potatoes.

With an electric mixer set at low speed, beat in the butter until it is melted. Add the milk, flour, baking powder, vanilla extract, almond extract, and salt and beat until the batter is smooth.

In a grease-free medium bowl, using clean beaters, beat the egg whites at low speed until they are foamy. Increase the speed to high and beat until soft peaks form. Continue beating and gradually add the sugar until stiff peaks form. Fold the egg whites into the sweet potato mixture. Transfer to the prepared baking dish.

In a small bowl, combine the brown sugar and cinnamon. Sprinkle it over the top of the soufflé. Bake for about 1 hour, until the top is browned and puffed. Serve immediately.

NUTRITIONAL CONTENT PER SERVING: **Calories: 324 Protein: 8 g**
Carbohydrates: 73 g Fat: 3.6 g Saturated fat: 0 g Cholesterol: 1 mg
Sodium: 450 mg Fiber: 6 g 10 percent calories from fat

Lemon-Blueberry Bread Pudding

Serves 8

Anything with the word "pudding" in it usually gets a bum rap for being fat-laden and over-rich. This bread pudding does not deserve such a reputation—it's fairly low in fat and just rich enough to be satisfyingly delicious. If the specialty grocery near you does not carry dried blueberries, use raisins instead. This would also be good with dried cranberries or dried cherries.

1¼ cups sugar, divided
3 tablespoons water
2 cups skim milk
2 large eggs
2 large egg whites
Grated zest of 1 lemon
1 teaspoon vanilla extract
⅛ teaspoon ground cinnamon
3½ cups cubed stale whole wheat bread (about 1-inch cubes)
½ cup dried blueberries or raisins

Preheat the oven to 350°F. Spray the inside of a 2-quart round baking dish with nonstick cooking spray.

In a small saucepan, bring ¾ cup of the sugar and the water to a boil over high heat. Stir to dissolve the sugar and make a caramel syrup. When the syrup comes to a boil, stop stirring and cook for about 3 minutes, occasionally swirling the pan by the handle, until the syrup has turned golden brown. Be sure to use a pot holder because the syrup is very hot.

Immediately pour the caramel into the prepared dish. Hold the dish with a thick kitchen towel or heavy oven mitts and quickly tilt and swirl it so that the caramel coats the inside evenly. Set aside.

In a small saucepan, heat the milk over high heat until small bubbles appear around the edges. Do not let the milk come to a full boil. It should only scald. Remove from the heat.

In a medium bowl, whisk the remaining ½ cup of sugar with the eggs, egg whites, lemon zest, vanilla, and cinnamon. Gradually whisk in the hot milk. Add the bread and blueberries or raisins. Pour this mixture into the caramel-coated baking dish.

Place the dish in a large baking pan, place the pan in the oven and add enough hot water to come halfway up the sides of the smaller dish. Bake for about 1 hour, until a sharp knife inserted into the center of the pudding comes out clean.

Remove the dish from the water bath and run a sharp knife around the inside to separate the pudding from the sides. Let stand for 30 minutes. Invert the dish onto a serving platter and unmold. Serve the pudding warm, at room temperature, or chilled.

NUTRITIONAL CONTENT PER SERVING: **Calories: 230   Protein: 7 g**
Carbohydrates: 47 g   Fat: 2 g   Saturated fat: 1 g   Cholesterol: 54 mg
Sodium: 173 mg   Fiber: 2 g   9 percent calories from fat

Chocolate Rice Pudding

I love chocolate pudding, and I like rice pudding a lot too. Perhaps you could say that indecision explains this version of both, which, depending on how you look at it, is a low-fat version of chocolate pudding or a wild version of rice pudding. If you're feeding a firehouse full of hungry firefighters, double the recipe (doubling also works if you're feeding a kitchen full of hungry teenagers). Be sure to use long-grain rice, not "minute" rice. Finally, if you leave a metal spoon in the pot while the rice cooks, it will prevent messy boil-overs.

4 cups skim milk
⅔ cup long-grain white rice
1 cup sugar, divided
Pinch of salt
½ ounce unsweetened chocolate, coarsely chopped
3 large egg whites
½ cup evaporated skim milk
1 teaspoon vanilla extract
1½ tablespoons all-purpose flour
½ cup raisins

In a large nonstick saucepan, bring the fresh milk, rice, ½ cup of the sugar, and the salt to a simmer over medium heat, stirring constantly. Reduce the heat to low and simmer for about 25 minutes, stirring often to prevent scorching, until the rice is tender. Add the chocolate and stir until melted.

In a medium bowl, whisk the egg whites, evaporated milk, vanilla, flour, and remaining ½ cup of sugar until smooth. Gradually whisk this mixture into the saucepan containing the rice. Whisking constantly, cook for 2 to 3 minutes, just until thickened; do not boil. Immediately transfer the pudding to a medium bowl and stir in the raisins.

Press a piece of plastic wrap directly onto the surface of the pudding. Cut several slits in the plastic wrap. Cool to room temperature and then refrigerate for at least 2 hours, until chilled. Serve chilled.

NUTRITIONAL CONTENT PER SERVING: **Calories: 252   Protein: 8 g**
Carbohydrates: 53 g   Fat: 1 g   Saturated fat: 1 g   Cholesterol: 3 mg
Sodium: 131 mg   Fiber: 1 g   5 percent calories from fat

Valerie's Angel Cake

Valerie Vautrin Gardinier, R.N.
Program Manager, Corporate Health Care Program
St. Vincent's Hospital
New York, New York

Serves 10

I met Valerie when I was hired by the Corporate Health Care Program at St. Vincent's as a fitness consultant for the employees. Her job is to set up health fairs for various corporations in New York City. In addition, she runs the Smoke Stoppers program for the hospital. Both endeavors mean she has done a great deal for the well-being of numerous New Yorkers. Being so aware of health issues, Valerie understands that some baked goods are more detrimental to overall health than others, but she also values the psychological benefits of baking and eating good food. This angel food cake is one of her favorites. Eat it with mixed berries or sliced peaches—it needs no frosting. Cake flour makes the cake as light as can be, but if you don't have any, substitute all-purpose, decreasing the amount by 2 tablespoons and adding that much cornstarch to the recipe. Be sure you don't buy self-rising cake flour.

1¼ cups sifted cake flour
1¼ cups sugar, divided
10 large egg whites, at room temperature
½ teaspoon fresh lemon juice
1 teaspoon cream of tartar
1 teaspoon vanilla extract
1 teaspoon almond extract

Position a rack in the lower third of the oven and preheat to 350°F.

In a medium bowl, sift the flour and ½ cup of the sugar together.

In the large bowl of an electric mixer set at low speed, beat the egg whites with the lemon juice until foamy. Add the cream of tartar, increase the speed to high, and beat until the whites form soft peaks. Gradually beat in the remaining ¾ cup of sugar until the whites form stiff peaks.

Fold the flour mixture into the egg whites, a third at a time. With the last addition, fold in the vanilla and almond extracts. Transfer the batter to an ungreased 10-inch angel food or tube pan. Bake for about 1 hour, until the cake has shrunk from the sides of the pan and a toothpick inserted into the cake comes out clean.

Turn the cake upside down to cool completely. Some pans have a long center tube or "feet" that raise the cake above the work surface. If not, balance the edges of the inverted pan on upside-down coffee mugs or insert the tube into the neck of a large soda bottle. When cool, run a sharp knife around the inside of the pan and the outside of the center tube to release the cake. Carefully ease the cake out of the pan and onto a serving plate.

NUTRITIONAL CONTENT PER SERVING: (1 serving = one 1-inch slice)
Calories: 161   Protein: 4 g   Carbohydrates: 35 g   Fat: 0 g   Saturated fat: 0 g
Cholesterol: 0 mg   Sodium: 56 mg   Fiber: 0 g   less than 1 percent calories
from fat

Oven Banana Pudding

Here I go again with bananas, but for good reason. They're full of potassium and are so naturally sweet that you need very little additional sugar to make a soul-satisfying pudding. Plus, this pudding is so fast and easy to make, you can whip it up at the drop of a hat—or between fire alarms.

3 ripe bananas
1⅓ cups skim milk
2 large eggs
4 large egg whites
½ cup sugar
¼ cup all-purpose flour
2 teaspoons vanilla extract
¼ teaspoon salt
2 tablespoons packed brown sugar
⅛ teaspoon ground cinnamon

Preheat the oven to 375°F. Spray an 11-by-7-inch glass baking dish with nonstick cooking spray.

Cut 2 bananas into large chunks and the remaining one into ½-inch-thick rounds. Arrange the sliced banana rounds in the bottom of the prepared dish.

In a blender, combine the banana chunks, milk, eggs, egg whites, sugar, flour, vanilla, and salt and process until smooth. Pour the mixture over the banana rounds and sprinkle with brown sugar and cinnamon.

$\mathbf{B}$ake for about 20 minutes, until the center of the pudding springs back when pressed lightly with a finger. Serve immediately.

NUTRITIONAL CONTENT PER SERVING: **Calories: 310   Protein: 12 g**
Carbohydrates: 61 g   Fat: 3 g   Saturated fat: 1 g   Cholesterol: 107 mg
Sodium 263 mg   Fiber: 2 g   9 percent calories from fat

Fire and Ice Two-Fruit Crisp

Serves 6

You can make this fruit crisp any time of year because apples are always available and the raspberries are frozen. Of course, nothing should stop you from making this with fresh raspberries in midsummer, when the fragile berries are in season. Crisps are quick-to-make desserts that are generally lower in fat than fruit pies. At our firehouse we eat this with frozen yogurt instead of the ice cream we used to eat with apple pie. The change has saved a lot of waistlines!

⅓ cup sugar
2 tablespoons all-purpose flour
2 teaspoons ground cinnamon, divided
4 tart apples such as Granny Smith, peeled, cored, and sliced ½ inch thick
One 10-ounce package frozen unsweetened raspberries (about 2 cups)
1 cup quick-cooking rolled oats
¼ cup packed brown sugar
¼ cup unsalted butter, softened

Preheat the oven to 350°F.

In a large bowl, combine the sugar, flour, and 1 teaspoon of the cinnamon. Add the apples and raspberries and toss well. Transfer to an ungreased 11-by-7-inch baking dish.

In a medium bowl, use a pastry blender or fork to combine the oats, brown sugar, butter, and remaining 1 teaspoon cinnamon to form a crumbly mixture. Sprinkle over the fruit.

$\mathbb{B}$ake for about 40 minutes, until the apples are tender and the top is browned. Serve warm or at room temperature.

NUTRITIONAL CONTENT PER SERVING: **Calories: 267   Protein: 3 g**
Carbohydrates: 46 g   Fat: 9 g   Saturated fat: 5 g   Cholesterol: 21 mg
Sodium: 4 mg   Fiber: 6 g   29 percent calories from fat

$\mathbb{B}$anana Dessert Smoothie

Serves 4

$\mathbb{S}$ometimes pouring a smooth, frothy drink into a tall glass is the best way to enjoy dessert. This thick banana smoothie is also a great afternoon pick-me-up or nutritious low-calorie breakfast. A similar recipe in a Spa Chiquita brochure inspired me to concoct this one.

3 ripe bananas
2 tablespoons lemon or lime juice
1 tablespoon honey
2 cups sparkling cider or 1 cup apple cider and 1 cup club soda
6 ice cubes
⅛ teaspoon grated nutmeg

$\mathbb{P}$ut the ingredients in a blender and blend at high speed until the mixture is creamy and frothy. Pour into chilled tall glasses and serve immediately.

NUTRITIONAL CONTENT PER SERVING: **Calories: 120   Protein: 1 g**
Carbohydrates: 31 g   Fat: 1 g   Saturated fat: 0 g   Cholesterol: 0 mg
Sodium: 4 mg   Fiber: 1 g   3 percent calories from fat

Firefighters Fat-Free Tapioca

By using skim milk and liquid egg substitute, I have eliminated the fat from tapioca pudding—a comfort food if ever there was one. I have to admit that this simple, old-fashioned dessert is my all-time favorite.

2¾ cups skim milk
⅓ cup sugar
¼ cup liquid egg substitute
3 tablespoons instant tapioca
1 teaspoon vanilla extract

In a medium saucepan, stir together the milk, sugar, liquid egg substitute, and tapioca. Let stand for 5 minutes. Bring to a boil over medium heat and cook for about 5 minutes, stirring constantly. Remove the saucepan from the heat and stir in the vanilla.

Transfer the pudding to a bowl and let cool slightly. Serve warm, at room temperature, or chilled.

NUTRITIONAL CONTENT PER SERVING: **Calories: 158   Protein: 8 g**
Carbohydrates: 30 g   Fat: 1 g   Saturated fat: 0 g   Cholesterol: 3 mg
Sodium: 115 mg   Fiber: 0 g   5 percent calories from fat

The Sweetest Fruit Compote

Serves 10

It takes a little patience to prepare this fruit compote, but once it is made, the natural sweetness of the fruit will satisfy any sweet tooth—without the addition of refined sugar, honey, or syrup. This dessert is very low in fat and contains zero cholesterol. I suggest buying the dried fruits from a health food store if possible. You can buy them in bulk, and they are less apt to be treated with preservatives.

15 ounces pitted prunes
9 ounces raisins
9 ounces golden raisins
8 ounces dried apricots
5 ounces dried pears

In a large bowl, mix together all of the dried fruit and add enough cold water to cover by ½ inch. Cover and refrigerate for 8 hours or overnight.

Pour the fruit and liquid into a large saucepan and bring to a boil over high heat. Reduce the heat to low and simmer for 30 minutes to 1 hour, until the fruit has softened to your taste.

Remove the saucepan from the heat and transfer the compote with its liquid to a serving bowl. Cover and refrigerate for at least 2 hours, until the compote is well chilled. Serve chilled.

NUTRITIONAL CONTENT PER SERVING: **Calories: 432   Protein: 5 g**
Carbohydrates: 114 g   Fat: 1 g   Saturated fat: 0 g   Cholesterol: 0 mg
Sodium: 14 mg   Fiber: 14 g   2 percent calories from fat

Noodle Pudding

Firefighter Anthony Reina

Fire Marshal, Queens Base

New York City Fire Department

Queens, New York (Retired to New Port Richey, Florida)

Serves 8

Noodle pudding is usually packed with high-fat cheese and eggs. This version is low in fat and cholesterol but nevertheless successfully transports you to the comfort zone.

8 ounces yolk-free egg noodles

1 cup fat-free cottage cheese

8 ounces fat-free whipped cream cheese product

1 cup nonfat sour cream substitute

1 cup liquid egg substitute

1 cup sugar

¼ cup margarine or butter, melted

1 teaspoon vanilla extract

¼ teaspoon ground cinnamon

Preheat the oven to 350°F. Spray a 13-by-9-inch baking dish with nonstick cooking spray.

Bring a large saucepan of lightly salted water to a boil, add the noodles, and cook for about 9 minutes, until they are just tender. Drain well.

In a medium bowl, whisk together the cottage cheese, cream cheese, sour cream, liquid egg substitute, sugar, melted margarine, and vanilla. Add the noodles and stir until they are well combined. Transfer the mixture to the prepared dish and sprinkle with cinnamon.

Bake for about 35 minutes, until the center is set. Serve hot, warm, or at room temperature.

NUTRITIONAL CONTENT PER SERVING: **Calories: 458   Protein: 25 g**
Carbohydrates: 65 g   Fat: 10 g   Saturated fat: 2 g   Cholesterol: 10 mg
Sodium: 253 mg   Fiber 2 g   19 percent calories from fat

Index